The Work of Creation

The Work of Creation

Cosmos, consciousness and the new sciences

FRANK AVRAY WILSON

COVENTURE LTD

London

First published in Great Britain by
Coventure Ltd, London

ISBN 0 904575 33 0

Cover illustration: Catherine Barnazet
Cover typography: Jutta Laing
Chapter-head illustrations: Frank Avray Wilson

Photoset by Red Lion Typesetters, London N5
and printed by
Redwood Burn Ltd
Trowbridge, Wilts.

Contents

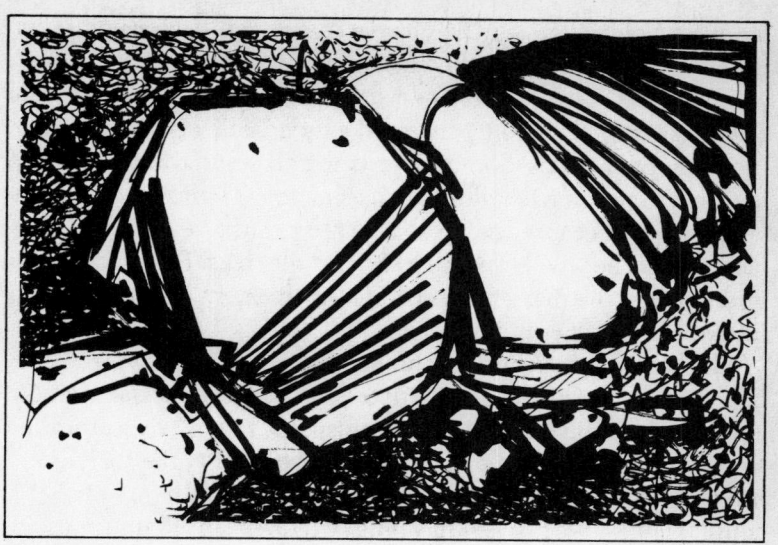

Introduction

Existence has become increasingly specialised, and, in its more chaotic aspects, torn in internal conflicts and warring oppositions of every kind. Possibly it is this schizoid trait in the modern world that has stirred the modern quest to see and be part of the whole. Whatever the reason, what was once a minority preoccupation among a few out-of-the-way thinkers and philosophers, has now grown to a widely shared quest, in league with the movements for an end to the devastation of nature and environment.

This new search for the whole as a largely cult concern, has been more passionate, idealistic and humanitarian than reasoned or scientific. But support is coming in now from science. This is encouraging, for although what people strive for intuitively and spontaneously is very important, possibly expressing some deep stirring in the communal mind, we exist in a civilisation set and ruled by science. As long as science is not brought into this quest for the whole, there is little chance that it will become an established drive in the body of civilisation.

So far, this concern with the whole by scientists has come from the physicists, inspired by the markedly holistic organisation and functioning of atoms. Some subjects which are in themselves rich in the evidence of wholeness, such as biology, are as yet not involved, possibly because these subjects are of such bewildering complexity that the wood cannot be seen for the trees. But as physics is undoubtedly the master science, its involvement in the subject is likely to be decisive.

The present official establishment viewing of nature and reality has proved extremely destructive. The surge of dissatisfaction, anger and criminality in the most prosperous industrial communities is partly the outcome of the long teaching that the Universe is humanly irrelevant and meaningless – that only material life counts. Unless we can feel meaning, which means finding a useful place for the human presence in nature, it seems likely that human beings on this planet will set about their own destruction in growing restlessness, hatred and violence. The human mind appears incapable of existing in a human way without such a belief. The most destructive defect in scientific viewing is the exclusion of the qualities of love, compassion, and altruism. Beauty and harmony are real and necessary constituents of a genuinely human existence. All of these are almost as important as food or shelter.

Any acceptable correction of this defect must not only find a natural place for such humanly indispensable beliefs, it must also respect the importance which science has placed on the material order. This would mean the very difficult reconciliation of the non-material and the material; a challenge which has so far seemed impossible in view of the prevailing cultural beliefs that all that is truly real must in some way be material.

The writer has come upon an alternative viewing of nature and reality which meets these requirements, thanks to a long sustained interest in a non-material aspect of nature: in its amazing and wonderful displays of art. This approach will rely on the evidence of nature's aesthetics, which has been almost completely neglected by science, for the very reason that it implies a non-material aspect of nature. Support will be sought in the strange discoveries of the new physics, the consequences of which many physicists prefer to avoid, so challenging are they to the establishment viewing.

This alternative does enable the unwhole, disjointed and schizoid viewing of reality to be seen as aspects of a natural enwholing, creative process. While this alternative is radically different from what most people believe to be valid and scientifically respectable, it is hoped that as the pieces fit, it will be judged as at least deserving further investigation. This small book is in fact an introduction to a very vast subject, many important aspects of which have only been very briefly touched upon. I hope to deal more fully with these in a later publication.

CHAPTER 1

Matter, and the new physics

Art and science are not easily reconciled, for the one appeals to feelings, emotions and intuitions which resist analysis and rational explanations, while the other depends entirely on reason and logic. Reconciliation has not usually attempted to reach a holistic, integrated solution, but rather a domination of art by science which necessarily entails its impoverishment.

Because science has been so successful in accounting for the material world, those aspects of nature which require an emotional and intuitive approach have been neglected. And yet, such aspects are most powerfully abundant and assertive if one's intuitive eye is opened to them. In failing to provide a satisfactory explanation of nature's art, science has left out of its account the most humanly important factors. This is the reason for the two-cultures split inherent in Western civilisation.

As art has been such a compelling feature of all culture and civilisation, one is entitled to expect that an explanation of the role of art in nature might have something important to say regarding both human art and the working of the Universe generally. It could be the key to the possible relevance of the human being in Creation; a relevance absent in the present scientific interpretation of reality.

This book provides such a reconciling view of nature's apparent duality in art. But as the aesthetic process cannot be reduced to the exclusively material and mechanical, it will be necessary to bring in a new, alternative approach to nature, one, nonetheless, seen as a part of the physical, self-consistent Universe hinted at by quite new events in the most matter-concerned of the sciences: physics.

In the past, such an alternative would have opened the doors wide to the supernatural, for what was not material could only be conceived in those terms. This is no longer the case. Physics itself has been obliged to accept a non-material foundation in nature, ever since the Michelson-Morley experiment at the turn of the century proved that there was no such thing as the assumed, all-unifying material background — the so-called aether of space.

Einstein found the way out of this dilemma by treating the non-material foundation of nature as a mathematical device: the continuum of space-time. A further feature of this continuum was described mathematically by Einstein as a variable 'curvature of space-time', based on non-Euclidian geometry. This could account for gravity, for the appearance of matter out of energy and for its disappearance according to the famous equation $E = mc^2$. Physicists, mathematicians, and rationalists in general, have been so relieved following the shock of the de-materialisation of reality, that they have been content to accept it while avoiding its revolutionary implications for the possible meaning of existence. But some famous philosopher scientists (more often astronomers than physicists), Eddington and Jeans in the thirties, and Sir Fred Hoyle today, have drawn attention to the essential feature of this situation, ie that the material world is of undoubted importance, but fundamentally, reality is not material. To say that it is mathematical is meaningless to the ordinary person. Yet the mathematics of Relativity theory has proved so successful (and has been so amply confirmed) one has to concede that the mathematical interpretation is not merely mathematical but refers to a real, existing aspect of physical reality, and to a core beyond the description of common-sense.

This seems to be an affront to common sense and intellect, for ever since the Greeks it has been insisted upon that reason, so close to common sense, is the ultimate means of understanding. The same ancient intellectual background has also insisted that ultimately reality is simple – a belief in simplicity reiterated as recently as the present century by such giants as Einstein. Unfortunately, the deeper one has gone into the working of nature, the more it has become evident that nature is extremely complicated. One can come to grips with this situation, but not by common understanding; extremely sophisticated symbolic procedures, such as mathematics, are necessary. Fortunately, this does not mean that the ordinary, non-mathematical person is precluded from understanding nature. Contrary to what has been long supposed, reason and intellect are not the only routes to understanding. Intuition, so long neglected and treated as primitive and unreliable, is now seen, in mathematics itself, as a very reliable accompaniment to knowledge: knowledge more felt and experienced than dissected and disassembled – a royal route to more holistic approaches to nature.

Provided science and mathematics touch into the roots of reality, the ordinary person can get the intuitive gist of what is happening in popular accounts of the subject. This may not be easy and is often demanding, but illumination can come, often quite suddenly and convincingly. Therefore, while the scientists may remain in their mathematical worlds, the ordinary person can, and should, endeavour to come to terms with the new revelations of nature in science. Although the non-material factor in question cannot be conceived by the intellect, it has to be accepted, and can be grasped intuitively. Once this is done, the approach to nature by the ordinary person is revolutionised. While scientists and mathematicians remain content with their technical elaborations, avoiding the practical consequences to everyday existence, ordinary people (thanks to the expert popularisers of these subjects now available) can draw the inferences affecting their lives. One such inference is that as a non-material aspect must now be accepted, the material world, and its changes and evolution in space and time, must in some way affect it. Otherwise, reality would be unwhole, fractured into two irreconcilable parts.

The great philosopher of science, Alfred North Whitehead, nearly a century ago emphasised that the material world not only emanates from the non-material, but that it must also affect the non-material. This results in an interaction which provides the material world with its evident non-material qualities. After decades of materialistic over-confidence, the more philosophically-minded scientists are once again reverting to this reconciliation of the material and the non-material, thereby paving the way to an enwholing view of reality and nature. Professor David Bohm of London University is a notable example of this trend.

It is now well understood how matter arises out of energy. Indeed, matter is energy organised in very special ways, and energy refers to the non-material, field aspect of physical reality. What is by no means clear, as yet, is how matter affects the non-material moiety of reality, and how such an effect can in return influence material events. In spite of this present absence of knowledge, it is logical to foresee that such an interaction must take place, and must be extremely important to the overall working of nature.

The reason for this impasse, temporary for sure, is the extreme difficulty experienced by scientists, philosophers and ordinary people in accepting the full reality of a non-material aspect of nature. Such an admission goes against the grain of Western culture, materialistic from its roots in ancient Greece and natively suspicious of the transcendental. So strong is this aversion, that it is felt preferable to ignore the reality of such qualities as beauty, wholeness, harmony, coordination and inspiration in nature and existence, rather than face the non-material admission which alone can account for them.

The reason why it is astronomers, rather than physicists or

other scientists, who have faced the reality of a non-material moiety in nature and the cosmos, is the fact that Relativity theory is particularly applicable to the vast masses of astronomical objects, and the inconceivably extensive space separating them. Relativity theory is much less useful to the physicist because the continuum of space-time, the expression of the non-material at the astronomical scale, is useless to the physicist dealing with entities and events occurring at a scale of millionths of a millimeter. The entities he deals with, if he is to be able to deal with them at all, have to be distinct and not continuous.

This could have been a situation of complete crisis, for penetration into matter, sooner or later, was bound to come upon the same non-material aspect which astronomers have encountered in the continuum of space-time. One should naturally expect that in the microphysical, subatomic level of the physicist, the non-material foundation would also be continuous. Ultimately, it most probably is continuous, for discontinuity is, in fact, a material property. What is timeless, spaceless and insubstantial must be continuous. It is here that one comes upon the most extraordinary provision on the part of nature, which has made the exploration of the microphysical world by the physicist possible. Nature has presented its microphysical continuity in a discontinuous manner!

Had the non-material aspect of atomic and subatomic events been continuous, there could have been none of the sensational advances of physics which have occurred in the past century. It is therefore truly astounding to find that as energy makes its presence felt in the world of substance, space and time, it does so in extremely small packets, known as quantas. Billions of them exist in every millimeter, and although entirely insubstantial, they exist in space, and so can be treated as distinct entities carried in the quite insubstantial waves of radiation. Thanks to this amazing grace and favour on the part of nature, the physicist can apply many of the laws of mechanics he has learnt about in the material world to these quantas: the strange foundation on which so-called quantum mechanics rests.

Typical of human arrogance and vanity, the earlier quantum physicists fooled themselves by seeing only one side of this, and assumed that nature and reality were at heart mechanical. In one sense, admittedly a very limited one, this is true, for these absolutely non-material quantas can be partly treated as mechanical entities. But it is a purely functional mechanism: a machinery without substance and material which makes no sense at all to common reason. Nonetheless, this paradox on the part of nature has enabled its exploration by the human intellect. In having reached the quarks and gluons, the human mind has probably come very close to the paradox: a truly amazing adventure, thanks to a barely believable concession on the part of nature, which should stir gratitude and humility rather than arrogance.

The non-material aspect of the microphysical world is dealt with by the field concept, which originated in the days of Faraday and Maxwell as a medium in which electromagnetic action could be seen to take place. At the time, this field was believed to be, in some remote sense, material, like the aether of space. But by the close of the 19th century, evidence was accumulating to suggest that the field could not be material – a suspicion confirmed by the Michelson Morley experiment. The *field* of quantum physics is a non-material, mathematically expressed feature, which like the continuum of space-time, must refer to some fundamental aspect of physical reality. One finds here how it is that physics, having come to the non-material core of reality, is afflicted with terms like 'fields' and 'particles' which have a material connotation. They were used not only because scientists hoped against hope that these non-material entities would in time be found to be in some sense material, but because words denoting non-material events barely exist in our language. This has come into being, let it be recalled, to deal primarily with the sensible, common sense world. In the deepest and most recent penetrations of physics into the probably ultimate world of quarks and gluons, physicists have at last been forced to abandon all pretexts of retaining a material hold on their terminology. They have resorted to purely qualitative terms, like colour and flavour, to define the totally insubstantial properties of the quark world.

Even the non-scientist must be aware that the continuum of relativity theory, and the field of quantum physics, must be aspects of the same thing: aspects of the universal, totally insubstantial and timeless substratum upholding the Universe. But up to now, rather surprisingly, the mathematics to unify these two insubstantialities has not been forthcoming. This is the most daunting failure in physics today. It casts a shadow on its otherwise fantastic successes. No doubt the necessary enwholing mathematic will in time appear. Like all else, mathematics continues to make sensational discoveries of its own. But this eventual success is likely to demand an entirely new, revolutionary way of looking at nature and reality, for which science is not yet ready.

But in spite of this shadow, quantum field theories – in their most recent form, known as quantum chromodynamics and able to tackle the quarks – are proving very successful. Particles composing the atom need no longer be treated as things; they can be handled as aspects of field. They are thus dealt with as effectively non-material entities, enabling their amazing metamorphoses to be instantaneously correlated. The field has in fact become a non-material creative matrix, in which entities can arise and be coordinated with other events and entities in a truly holistic way. Furthermore, by bringing in advanced mathematical notions of symmetry (the delight of all mathematicians) it has been able to predict the existence of particles not known at the time, but subsequently discovered; an encouraging confirmation that such mathematics is truly dealing with reality.

One can expect that possibly in the near future, such is the resourcefulness of the human mind, that mathematical ways will be found to explain and confirm the manner in which the non-material and the material aspects of reality interact in a concerted, whole-insisting manner. Then we will at last have a holistic interpretation of nature and reality. One can predict the broad lines which this ultimate resolution will take. As matter arises from the field, thanks to the particular organisation of energy in the form of quarks, particles, and then of atoms and molecules, such entities retain an ability to influence the field. They organise it, in purely functional, non-material ways, corresponding to the events occurring in the material world. So as matter exists, functions, experiences and evolves, its experience is not lost, but accumulated beyond space and time. This accumulation can provide the expertise, supervision and theme so evident in nature and evolution.

Furthermore, as the field is worked upon by matter, so qualities inherent in the field are exploited and developed, and in time, incorporated in the forms, things and creatures of the material world. Necessarily, such field qualities will be different but analogous to it in aesthetics, wholeness, harmony and beauty.

Early in my search for an explanation of nature's great art making, it seemed to me that only such an ingenious organisation of matter could account for the material order, for the distinctive qualities of aesthetic order, and for the evidence of supervision and inspiration in nature. If nature is in fact organised in such a way, one would expect it to begin in a very random manner, with no evidence of the field qualities in the material forms of nature. But as evolution proceeded and field involvement became more organised, material experience accumulated and was in some way sorted out. The playback into the material world of such field qualities would have increased and become ever more manifest in nature.

This indeed is found to be the case, for the aesthetics of nature has increased as evolution has gained momentum. Apart from the primordial crystalline forms of matter, which express the inherent aesthetics of atomic order, the forms of things and creatures were at first uncouth and ungainly. Nature's art only came into being, suddenly and overwhelmingly in Cretaceous times, some seventy million years ago. As life appeared on earth some three thousand million years ago, it needed that length of time for the aesthetic field expertise to be properly worked out. One can begin to understand why evolution has needed such a long timing.

Here then is the circumstantial evidence that some such creative interaction between material and non-material aspects of nature is a feature of reality. The way to a completely different interpretation of nature and reality opens up. For instance, the beauty of the crystalline order, so striking in mineral crystals, indicates that beyond appearances there lie protoforms or archetypes which become expressed in the existence and organisation of matter — archetypes which are most conveniently traced to the field, a fascinating subject to which we will return.

Another consequence which follows from an alternative viewing of nature is that the mind, and in fact the entire evolution of life and of the nervous system, can be understood as a progressive exploitation of the field involvement, playing back into the molecular systems. Cells, tissues, organs and living forms and communities of living organisms provide the visible evidence of field qualities: in *vitality*, in the wholeness of things, in their beauty and in the evidence of supervision, coordination and inspiration everywhere in nature.

If the nervous system and the brain and mind are interpreted as a very special exploitation of the field, then emotions and feelings can also be understood as field-derived qualities, made evident by very special living systems. So consciousness is itself a field-referant phenomenon. It follows that it should be no surprise that such a conscious mind should come to an understanding of what nature is about. Mind and nature meet on common ground: that of the universal field.

CHAPTER 2

The archetypes of nature

The admission that nature contains a perfectly natural, non-material aspect, has enabled an admittedly very rough sketching of the way matter – the unique creative material of the Universe – has managed to bring into being the multiplicity of created things from nebulae, stars and planets to living organisms. As we are part of this creativity, and have been equipped with sensitive organs to behold it in its material manifestation, we naturally assume that the work of nature is as we see it: material and substantial. But if the sketch of matter's way of working is correct, then this marvellous appearance of things has been brought into being so that the field can become organised. In believing that the material world is in itself the aim and end of nature's creativity, we have missed the very gist of it. This is the source of science's infirmity in the past.

This inference should be kept well in mind as the material ways of nature's creativity are investigated; for these ways are so fascinating, so marvellous and ingenious, that it is easy to become spellbound by them and to forget what nature is really about. Perhaps ultimate reality in Creation refers to the non-material moiety, not to the material, hard as this must be for us to grasp and accept. Yet it is a conclusion which the greatest thinkers on the subject had reached long before the advent of science. Science in its more recent advances has merely restored and confirmed a very ancient idea.

Great scientist philosophers like Jeans and Eddington, Einstein and many others, have had no hesitation in proclaiming that visible material reality cannot be the aim and end of the Creation. Reality must transcend matter, which in the language of the new physics means that nature is most real in its field aspect. The fact that matter, and its long and laboured evolution, has been indispensable for the parallel exploitation and evolution of the field, should not be allowed to depress us, or cast contempt on our material nature and life in a very material world. Without a doubt, this material order has been indispensable for the exploitation of the Universe's transcendental, field aspect.

We can now look a little more closely at the way the Janus-faced organisation of matter has enabled nature to work in its ingenious creative ways. In the first place, one must suppose that the non-material aspect of the Universe – one can call it the universal field – possesses inherent timeless organisational potentialities. A potentiality is no more than a tendency which becomes real only when it is organised and made to function. A potentiality thus differs fundamentally from a prelaid plan, like that of an engineer or architect which preexists the actual building or making of a machine. At most, these potentialities of the field can be thought of as insubstantial codes, which become real only as they are decoded.

Such potentialities have in fact been proposed in the new cosmology as a *pregeometry* – necessarily transcendental and field referent. This has acted as a constraint on the manifestation of energy in space and time, and so ensured that the Universe came into being in a very special way. Since the Big Bang some twelve thousand million years ago, it has subsequently expanded and evolved also in ways which completely dismissed the chanceful viewing of the Creation in past science.

One can observe with interest the groping now going on in theoretical physics to trace the creative in nature to field characteristics beyond space and time; gravity to supergravity and symmetry (that ultimate test of order in nature) to supersymmetry. The great Heisenberg affirmed that the still missing overall symmetry in the constituents of atoms, so clearly impingeing in the field, will ultimately be traced to a transcendental, metaphysical level.

The constituents of atoms, electrons, positrons, neutrinos and the quarks, out of which the nuclear particles are made, can be conceived as only existing in space and time in one aspect of their being. The other non-material aspect, made apparent in their wave-characteristics, refers to the field. This means that every particle has both a localised aspect and a non-localised aspect. An electron, for instance, is both here and now in association with a given atom, as well as having a repercussion throughout the Universe.

Either of these aspects can be accentuated at the sacrifice of the other (according to the Heisenberg principle) which means that a particle can be more massive and more involved in the material world than others. A few are barely involved at all, as in the case of the neutrino which is so slightly materially involved that it passes right through the planet as if it were not there at all. This provides nature with the means of acting in a more, or less, material way; a facility which has no doubt enabled it to create the material world, and at the same time, enabled this material world to create the ever more organised and versatile exploitation of the field.

This variable material and non-material involvement also means that nature can concentrate on isolated, localised processes, while at the same time keeping an overall, thoroughly holistic control of the Universe. That the Universe is a unity, with its contents, the nebulae and stars wonderfully spaced out with astounding regularity, cannot be doubted any more; and only a sustaining overall field influence, working through gravity, can possibly ensure this.

As for the localised concentrations of nature's creativity in material things and living organisms, isolation is only apparent and superficial. For the field involvement of all matter means that at the fundamental level in all things and creatures, there is unity. This transcends the Einstein limit of the speed of light applied to the space-time continuum only, so that the Universe is instantaneously self-unifying. This moving fact is expressed in a new principle: the Non-locality principle of quantum theory. This 'here and now' combined with the 'everywhere' and 'all time' is illustrated strikingly by the quarks in all the fundamental constituents of matter. Quarks are undoubtedly localised in particular atoms, but their universal field reference is so dominant, that to isolate a quark would entail the dismantling of the entire Universe, as the physicist Feynman has speculated.

The way in which nature has managed to combine these two apparently opposite qualities, i.e. localisation and universality, is by ceaselessly vibrating between the field, space and time: an in-and-out vibration which occurs in all matter at a rate of billions of times per second. Judged from the world of space and time, this is equivalent to a repeated disappearance of matter and its reappearance. Over half a century ago, Weyl interpreted this as a ceaseless recreation of the Universe, which simply does not exist continuously. We are here touching on an explanation as to why nature expresses itself in its first step into space and time discontinuously. This is so in order that the connection with the all-sustaining universal field can be maintained; and it is a further indication of how matter emerges out of the field, and in reverse, organises the field in parallel with all its changes and happenings.

Electrons and quarks are primordial expressions of the field in space and time, largely still field determined. But the way in which they become organised into atoms, must be determined by special field potentialities, ensuring that they are organised to form the 92 naturally occurring atoms or elements. Such potentialities can be imagined as protoforms, or archetypes of the very first order, for it is out of these 92 elements that all the material substances of nature are made. Such protoforms or archetypes possess evident self-constraints which not only limit the kinds of different atoms found in the Universe, but also the constraints on their interreaction. This in turn determines the different material objects and organisms which arise through evolution. As we shall see, the result of such a cumulative constraint has created a unique kind of Universe. Its programming also allowed a creature with a large, conscious brain, to develop and become the first creature to give conscious feedback.

These cues to the organisation and evolution of the material world, traceable to the archetypes of the field, are not crudely deterministic. Their influence is in fact extremely weak and subtle, requiring aeons of time to have any noticeable effect; and then this effect can be wide ranging and exploratory in a virtually random manner. This means that nature does not create in a linear way, as do engineers and architects. But in view of the persistence of the archetypes over aeons of time, a theme sorts itself out and becomes ever more assertive and distinctive, traceable to the archetypes of the field.

This is not the way we as human beings set about doing things. We make plans, and then follow out their directions as precisely as possible, which no doubt explains why it has taken such a long time for people to realise that evolution, over aeons of time, is nature's essential creative method. Although complicated and indirect to the point of being confusing, we simply have to accept that this is how nature has chosen to operate – most probably because it could not work in any other way.

It is of interest to note that Darwin struck upon a most important feature of nature's creativity: natural selection, as the means of eliminating what he termed the 'unfit', and allowing the 'fit' to survive and dominate the scene of Creation. Where he, and science in general have gone wrong, is to suppose that natural selection is blind, purely a matter of chance. It may indeed be largely chanceful, but given sufficient time – and there is no shortage of that in the Universe – a theme does work through, originally inspired, and no doubt sustained, by field archetypes. So natural selection can work just as effectively in the inorganic world, as it more evidently does among living organisms.

But natural selection, as we will find out, is only one aspect of nature's way of ensuring that the creative potentialities inherent in the field are in time realised. A far more important aspect, one which is directly creative, is due to the amassing of matter's experience and expertise – as an accumulation of information in the field – sorted out in appropriate ways under the influence of the field archetypes. In Darwin's time, there were no practical analogies of such a way of working. Computer and information theories, now highly resolved and elaborate, provide an excellent analogy of this process occurring in nature: the means of nature's accumulation of expertise and its eventual playback as a directive to evolution in space and time.

It may be thought that computer technology vindicates the mechanical approach to such problems, and it might seem that the success of computers puts the equivalent attempts on the part of nature in an inferior light, for the calculating and memorising abilities of computers far exceed those of the human brain. But this is a misinterpretation of the situation, for all such technologies, depending as they do on electromagnetic processes, involve the field. Indeed, compared to the subtleties achieved by living molecular systems, made evident in the holism of the living organism and in the creative range of the mind, present computer achievements are rudimentary and infantile. Nonetheless, looked at in the right way, they do provide a useful analogy of an important aspect of nature's way of working and creating e.g. storing of information, feedback and eventual playback, all done against a most subtle guidance of the field archetypes.

The biologist, Waddington, made an interesting suggestion in the otherwise baffling, highly deterministic and evidently superintended development of the embryo. He proposed that 'creodes' provided this overall supervision and coordination. Although he avoided definitely stating that his creodes were transcendental to the actual business of embryological development, it is evident that they can only make sense if they are so treated. This means that the creode is in fact what we have been calling an archetype or protoform. Waddington noted that a striking feature of life is its ceaseless throbbing, pulsation and shuffling at the ultramicroscopic level. Although often pictured as static, geometric objects in textbooks, the molecules of life are in fact ceaselessly and most dynamically agitated. He saw in this a truly creative tool. The ceaseless agitation at the molecular level provided the opportunity for the creodes to pick out the activities that mattered, like balls in a pin game falling into the right holes. Random agitation, archetypical influences and time, therefore, provide the determinism one finds in life.

One can apply this model more widely, seeing in the exuberance of life forms, in their amazing fantasmagora (superficially so wasteful and aimless) the means whereby the faint and discreet potentialities of the field, in the guise of archetypes, are given the chance to select the appropriate situations. Each situation is best suited to the immediate and future prospects of a particular organism, whilst taking into account the vast accumulated expertise of its evolutionary past. An ingenious creative method indeed, which makes the usual human way of doing things elemental and limited.

CHAPTER 3

The creative field and 'pregeometry'

Although physicists have avoided discussing the non-material aspect of the field, its physical reality can be very easily demonstrated. The electromagnetic field is active in a complete vacuum, and when one recalls that the 'aether of space' has been dismissed by physics itself, there should be no doubt regarding the existence of fields.

For convenience, some field-involving phenomena can be looked upon as localised. In an electromagnetic field, for instance, the effects fall off as inversely proportional to the distance, so that at some distance away the magnetic field influence can be ignored. But in theory, the effect of a magnet is universal. As mathematicians cannot deal with infinities, they have gone out of their way to find ingenious devices for avoiding this factor in their calculations.

But all events which impinge in the field have a universal reference, so that besides the convenience of localised field phenomena, one has to accept the reality of a universal field in which the Universe has its instantaneous being and which assures its unity. As the classical belief in localisation and accurate timing are challenged, strange phenomena become possible.

It is such intimations, inherent in quantum theory, which so disturbed Einstein, for they challenged his lingering classical conception of an orderly Universe. Accordingly he devised an experiment, with the help of some colleagues, which could resolve whether such intimations were real, or flaws in quantum theory. It is only quite recently that the means of carrying out such an experiment have become available, and the experiment so performed confirms that interactions between certain particles occur instantaneously, irrespective of the distance separating them. This confirmation of the already mentioned Non-locality principle of quantum theory is a subject to which we shall return. The limit which Einstein has set to the material world – the energy equivalent of the speed of light – thus turns out to be arbitrary. Nature and cosmos extend functionally beyond the limits of material existence.

Because the intellect insists so strongly that only the material, mechanical world can be properly real, the Non-locality principle, in spite of having been confirmed experimentally, is extremely difficult to accept. How can such an unprincipled trait be reconciled with the firm orderliness of the material world? The answer must be that for almost all the time, much, much longer than the lifetime of an individual, material orderliness triumphs. But every now and again, field events affect the material world in a very subtle manner, but sufficiently to ensure that it evolves one way rather than another. The Non-locality principle ensures that when that does happen, the effect can be far reaching.

This implies that although chance rules for almost all of the time, it is nonetheless occasionally challenged, events in nature receive a discreet shove in a particular direction. Were it not for the insistence, inbuilt in scientific materialism, that the Universe is an accidental production, this discreet guidance in nature would be more generally recognised in the amazing fact of evolution, in the coherence of ecology and in the orderly interdependence of the Universe generally. So while many physicists dogmatically insist that quantum events are entirely ruled by chance (for instance, the 'decay' of an atom is entirely unpredictable in the material world), this appears to be so only because observation does not cover a sufficient span of time; and because science has not yet come round to tracing decisions in nature to a matter-transcending aspect; an event which Heisenberg said would have to happen before the orderliness of nature was completely resolved.

The distinctiveness of the creative material of the Universe is expressed in the orderly relationship between the atoms of the 92 elements, from hydrogen to uranium, conveniently summarised in the periodic table of school chemistry texts. Fifty years ago, it was assumed that these differences between the elements were fortuitous and had no role to play in an overall scheme of Creation. Although less than a quarter of these elements are involved in life making, uses are increasingly being found for others in geological and astronomical activities. For example, in the role of certain metallic elements accumulating in supernovae, responsible for their explosion and the subsequent insemination into being of stars, such as the sun.

The settings of the atoms are such that quite minor variations would have ruled out the formation of nebulae and stars, and thus the eventual emergence of planetary life. Minor differences in the bonding powers of carbon, nitrogen, oxygen and other life-indispensable elements would have blocked the formation of the gigantic and versatile molecules on which life depends. The very special properties of substances such as water, are such that they could not be the result of chance. In support of such providence cosmologists are now proposing the so-called Anthropic Principle. This testifies, in scientific terms, that the Universe is especially geared to life and mind making by means of nature's special creative method: evolution. There could be no more dramatic reversal of the former chance-ridden picture of nature and cosmos.

The differences between the constituents of the nuclei of atoms, protons and neutrons etc is now known to be due to differences in the organisation of six quarks; and the versatile properties of these quarks can but be due to creative, organising potentialities invested in the field. Some cosmologists and physicists such as J.A. Wheeler of Princeton have accordingly been speculating that the field must consist of a ceaselessly churning, vibrating creative flux possessing, nonetheless, a sustaining dynamic patterning referred to as the 'pregeometry' of the Universe. Evidently it is this 'pregeometry' which is ultimately responsible for the very special features of matter, of the entire Universe. The 'pregeometry' is an aspect of the archetypes. The influence of this 'pregeometry' in space and time is extremely weak, requiring aeons of time for any noticeable effect upon the course of evolution. It is this weakness which accounts for nature's groping, experimental and often wasteful way of working, necessitating a ceaseless natural selection of the 'fit' from the 'unfit'. But extremely weak as it shows itself in the material world, it must possess a remarkable expertise, for given a timing of thousands of millions of years it has managed to pull off the virtual miracle of life and mind.

In the establishment scientific view of nature, evolution works purely by chance. This scenario has been dramatically changed recently as it has become widely appreciated that natural selection of random gene mutation, important as it undoubtedly is for bringing about change and adaptation, cannot account for the creatively new in evolution. Furthermore, since inorganic matter evolves as well as living matter, evolution must be a general principle, and any theory which can only account for the one without the other, must be defective. Indeed, this is the indication of the inadequacy of Darwin's theory of natural selection, for the principle, while undoubtedly important in the living world, has no application in the physical world.

While physicists are exploring the aspects of nature beyond substance, making revolutionary suggestions in the process regarding the nature of life and mind, biologists and psychologists remain mostly unconcerned with the revolution in progress. This may well be due to a psychological incompatibility, for while physics depends entirely on mathematics, life does not yield to a mathematical approach. A recent attempt by Sheldrake to show a transcendental supervision in biology (such essentially biological theories have been proposed from time to time over the past century) fails to make use of the unitary basis that physics is now providing. If the aesthetic contribution is added – here again, physicists and mathematicians are better aware of its value than biologists – most of the presently inexplicable features of nature fall into place.

CHAPTER 4

A creative theme

In the establishment viewing evolution has no theme, no object-ive. A worm can be as efficiently adapted as the human being and count as much in the random scale of things. In the past, any sug-gestion of a theme in evolution implied a supernatural interven-tion, and therefore, understandably, was opposed by science, for an indispensable dogma of science is that nature is self-consistent. Whatever comes into being must do so by natural law. Science has not denied a creative act by some supreme power beyond under-standing, but it has insisted that such a power has made use of natural means exclusively. As T.H. Huxley put it, if there is a supernatural world, it must be shown to operate naturally.

Newton's mechanical laws controlling the movement of the heavenly spheres opened the way to an exclusively mechanistic interpretation of nature. As machines cannot be conceived as arising on their own, so most people assumed that the Creator Deity had set the heavenly machine working, in such a way that it could continue to do so without intervention. But many rationally-minded people hoped that the time would come when the manner in which a purely mechanical Universe had come into being could be shown to be purely random, so dismissing the need for an original Creator. Darwin was so acclaimed, because the mechanical operation of natural selection appeared to provide such an explanation in the most complicated aspect of the Universe: the realm of life.

At the time, the inorganic realm was ignored, as it was believed to be elemental, and would in due course be quite simply explained. So an explanation of life's evolution seemed to solve the problem of an accidental, exclusively mechanical and material Universe. With further investigation, the inorganic has shown itself to be as complex and as remarkably coordinated as the world of life. The present concepts of star functioning are akin to the organic processes of life. So even if life was explained mechanically by Darwin's theory, there remained the challenge of an overall explanation of the inorganic, of the Universe as a whole. The majority of people who have given sufficient thought to this problem would probably agree today that the prospects of a purely mechanistic explanation can be ruled out. At the same time, Darwin's theory, amplified by the discovery of genes and mutation, has increasingly shown itself inadequate to account for the truly new and creative in evolution. As a result, science is back to square one, possessing no overall ideas as to how the Universe has come into being, and how it has subsequently evolved.

But the recent discovery of the ingenius balancing of forces of the atomic order has revived a hope that nature may be able to work out its own theme, given the way the Universe has been programmed from the start. This does not account for the original programming, but that can be taken for granted; it is sufficient to be able to provide a coherent account of the evidence of a creative theme in nature and evolution. In searching for clues as to how nature has managed to develop its own creative theme, one can begin with the already mentioned subject of crystallisation – the simplest expression of order made visible in nature. As soon as the Universe cooled sufficiently following the Big Bang, matter began to sort itself out and to crystallise in the equisitely beautiful forms of ice crystals, in such minerals as sulphur and other primordial materials.

Mechanically-minded crystallographers have attempted to account for such crystallisation by purely mechanical principles. Such principles undoubtedly apply, but as the American physicist Cantore pointed out, at the microlevels where crystals form, the molecular and atomic tumult is so intense that no simple stacking hypothesis, of the kind that one often finds in text books, is acceptable. The first stackings to form would be immediately destroyed, a subject I dealt with in my book, *Crystal and Cosmos* (1977). In other words, there must be a superintendent form-coordinating force able to insist that the particular crystal forms result, and such guidance cannot possibly be in the welter of agitating atoms and molecules. It has to be a superintendent, transcendental directive.

From what has already been said, such a directive is to be traced to the protoforms or archetypes of the field. No doubt these are quite simple to start with, at the dawn of the Universe. But as matter crystallised in intergalactic space, on countless cooling planets throughout the Universe, so a crystallising expertise accumulated in the field, universally available to guide crystallisation wherever it occurred. In the Universe today, after some twelve thousand million years of existence and accumulated experience, crystallisation is extremely efficient. Billions of crystallising units are correctly assembled, per second, in the formation of a crystal. It follows that matter's long evolution has established virtually every possible crystal form as a field organisation, starting with the original protoforms or archetypes. This accounts for the hundreds of visibly different and complex forms which a single substance or mineral, like calcite for instance, can assume.

A most important characteristic of the activity of these very first inorganic archetypes, is the startling beauty, symmetry and harmony of their productions. Few things are as beautiful as the choicest pieces of minerals, surpassing in every aesthetic criterion, the productions of human sculptors. So one can conclude that as the archetypes operate, guiding the formations of things in space and time, the guidance carries a strong aesthetic loading. This supports the hypothesis, necessarily more popular among artists than scientists, that nature is fundamentally a work of art, rather than a machine.

A study of crystals shows that the primordial archetypes must have been akin to the Platonic solids, except that these are usually pictured in strictly precise geometric forms. The archetypes, to the very limited extent that one can imagine them at all, must be inherently dynamic, ceaselessly quivering. As they are field entities, any direct representation of these archetypes is completely ruled out, although some of the more vital, modulated geometric forms one finds in the visual arts may give some idea of them.

It is on these limited number of primordial crystallising archetypes that the crystallising experience of nature, over aeons of geological time, has elaborated all the possible variations of crystalline form. A well-known attempt in Germany in the last century to catalogue all the possible crystalline form of minerals, ran into several volumes and tens of thousands of drawings. Each of these elaborations on the primordial archetypes became archetypes in their own right, themselves subject to further elaboration. But in the case of crystals, the possible number may be limited by the combinational constraints between atoms. It cannot be overemphasised that these crystallising archetypes are universal. On any planet anywhere in the universe, they are as instantaneously available to guide the formation of crystals as they are for a chemist synthetising some new substance in his laboratory. Although endless synthetics are possible, their crystals are bound to form according to some appropriate archetype already elaborated upon by matter's universal experiencing, accumulated in the universal field.

It is also important to emphasise that the visible crystal is necessarily a symbolic representation of the relevant archetypes; a rather rigid and geometric symbolisation owing to the way billions upon billions of atoms build up onto the visible world. This precise geometric form also agrees with the ideals of the intellect, for precision and simplicity, which accounts for the fascination of crystallography. Under its visual restrictions, amounting to deception, what underlies the visible crystal is a throbbing, palpitating organisation of archetypes.

This involvement of field archetypes in the formation of crystals illustrates how growth and form take place in nature generally. The potentialities of the field provide elemental protoforms which subsequently become elaborated and diversified by evolution, and thereby provides the wealth and variability, combined with evident underlying motifs and themes, of inorganic and organic nature. Life is constantly increasing this variability. Inorganic things also show an arresting ability to creative expression, for example in crystals, geological structures and in astronomical entities.

In the case of living organisms, there would appear to be a hierarchy of archetypes at work: some providing the general underlying structures and functions, others taking the work of creation further by providing the variability of organisms, even within a species. For instance, insects and worms show a frequent segmentation which probably refers to archetypes first at work in the earlier phases of organic evolution, whereas higher animals show a repeated display of limbs, organs and other structures, which imply a widely acting set of archetypes. The connection between the archetypes and the genes should be evident. Indeed, these directive bundles of DNA can be looked upon as the executives of the archetypal influences. They probably evolved separately and were arranged into the earliest organisms by assembling archetypes.

The famous biological classic, d'Arcy Thomson's *Growth and Form*, attempted to catalogue the visible connection between the forms of growth and development in living organisms and physical and mechanical forces. This fascinating study has intrigued many in the arts as well, but the connections remain unaccounted for. For example, that a drop of water should splash into the form of a medusa rules out any possible physical connection, except pure chance. Bringing in the archetypal concept, however, does make it possible to envisage that some particular archetype is called in. It would account for the medusal shape organising the molecules of the medusa in much the same way as the physical forces forming the shape of the splash. The connection is thus field referent, not to be found at the material level. Archetypes, it will be remembered, are universally and instantaneously available to influence the genesis of form and structure. In the organic world they act through special structures like genes; in the inorganic order, they work directly upon atoms and molecules, as in the case of crystals – probably by the intermediacy of quarks, electrons and neutrinos. The archetypal influence reaches its culmination in the evolution of the nervous system and the brain. As the most evolved form of matter, they can be looked upon as the most effective field-connected material systems available, raising a supervision and inspiration, which was formerly carried out by genes, to a quite new level of organisation. This enables the utmost organisation of the field itself, fed back from the experience of living.

This culminating achievement of matter in the nervous system and brain can therefore serve as the focalising point of the whole of biological evolution and creation. Indeed, rather than interpret the different organs and tissues as determining the evolution of the nervous system, one should see the entire expression of life, in cells, tissues organs and organisms, as the means to bring into being a nervous system and brain, culminating in the humanised primate brain.

Therefore, to judge this field involvement of nature's creativity at its highest point, the psyche is the most likely to provide the clues for its symbolic understanding. The exploration of psyche most useful for this is that initiated by Jung. From a study of dream imagery, Jung concluded that certain images referred to an aspect of the mind's domain which transcended the individual psyche. This was the collective unconscious, which can be interpreted as the field involvement of human minds – a sort of automatic universal pooling. The archetypes which Jung discovered are necessarily highly complex entities, overlapping into hierarchies of levels in the field, rising from the totally abstract into the variously embodied and figurative, as they become adapted to serve existence. Tracing back such archetypes to their abstract roots, one comes upon the protoforms which stem from the timeless potentialities of the field, back through the entire evolutionary history of life, of the Universe itself.

Just as the crystalline state can be considered as an elaboration of some primordial archetypal potentialities invested in the universal field (possibly preceding the creation of the Universe), so the highly evolved Jungian archetypes, acting at the level of the human mind, can be understood as these primordial archetypes worked upon by the entire evolution of the human species. They are truly the most fundamental constituents of the psyche, and like the quarks, both localised and individualised, as well as universal.

Thanks to the elaboration of archetypes in the course of evolution, all the multitudes of life's components within organisms, between organisms and environments, and, indeed, between planetary systems, are both localised, and universally unified – a property particularly evident in the mind. The universal field has, from the start, provided the Universe with the means of unification and wholeness. This has been effectively exploited by the evolution of the archetypes, ensuring that the visible appearances of separation are fundamentally reconciled in a universalising unity. Had Emmanuel Kant sensed these all-unifying forces at work everywhere in nature, and beyond appearances, he would not have been so terrified by the apparent immense separation of the stars. Such a separation is instantaneously reconciled at the field level, to which the intuitive mind has access.

This sense of unity and wholeness is not entirely beyond the common appearances. To the extent that the field influences have been made manifest in things and creatures in symbolic ways, in their evident wholeness, harmony, beauty and vitality, one can say that the underlying unity is actually seen and experienced in the ordinary world. It is by ignoring this intuitive approach, by which we sense the transcendental quality in things, that science has missed the essential components in reality: components most closely attuned to the human presence in the scheme of Creation. It is here that the arts score over science.

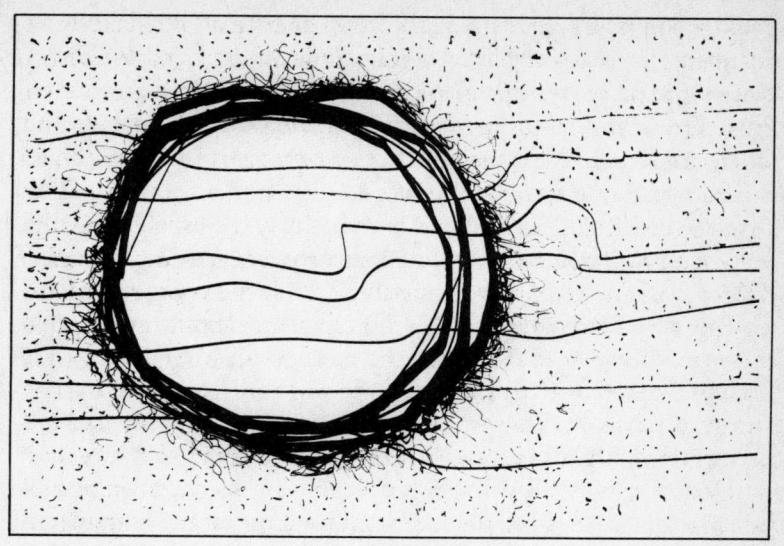

CHAPTER 5

The evidence of guidance

The primordial archetypes, and their progressive elaboration in the course of evolution, is nature's theme; the thread of twisting and winding determinism behind its labours and groping. In a very striking way, the sources of inspiration in all the arts provide a close analogy to this, for inspiration in the arts undoubtedly comes when the archetypes are intuitively touched into. These occasional lightning shafts of sudden inspiration in prolonged, groping, staggered and frustrated efforts are so close to nature's way of working.

Determinism in nature may be obscured by the domination of the groping, the wasted efforts and the profligate diversity, for while the artist can eliminate his failures as he proceeds, nature cannot always do so. Much of the clutter of failed experiment, of dead ends, lie all around. The apparently random forces at work in geology are now known to be the consequence of intrinsically co-ordinated activities in plate tectonics and continental drift. Underlying the apparently unprincipled creative efforts of nature, there is a sustaining and mounting orderliness and self-found inspiration, which the sensitive, attuned eye can perceive. And once perceived, it is indeed found to be everywhere.

In the late fifties, when I was both actively painting and searching for an explanation of the evident inspiration and guidance in nature's art and in human creative effort, I came upon a passage in a writing by Herbert Read (which I have since been unable to re-trace) in which Read described the method of subliminal meditation discovered by a poet, whereby he was able to observe the constituting forms of 'things' and 'creatures'. To my joy and surprise, I found that this could be easily done by practised relaxation in the subliminal interval between waking and sleep, when one can just manage to precariously remain a spectator to the spontaneous, creative magic of the mind. Such a state cannot be sustained, for the least overlap by one tendency or the other, sleep or waking, and the spell is broken. But the recollected fragments provide a most fascinating insight into the activity of archetypes, as numinous, dream-like forms – luminous, sparkling, effervescent, spectral, drift upon the precarious scene.

Such protoforms are truly 'alive', for they not only palpitate and tremble, but metamorphose readily in endless variations to form elaborate, ever more complex entities. By noting down these forms, one comes upon the constituents of the effective archetypes behind all created things and creatures. For instance, 'head-like' entities join with repeated segmented strips to form insect-like forms; darting trajectories join with trembling focalised circles and spirals to form the most fantastic shell-like creatures. And cell-like forms abound in all possible variety and profusion. Indeed, one gets the impression that in this strange creative fantasmagoria, no doubt occurring ceaselessly in every mind, far more creative possibilities are struck into than have been realised in nature. Having been long fascinated by crystals and minerals, I have come upon 'crystalline' entities never seen in existence; truly fantastic, magical forms metamorphosing into the floral and the pyrotechnical. It is here, in this fascinating half-world, that the fantasmagoria of created things and creatures can be accounted for as a realised, manifested and expressed moment in this ceaseless metamorphosis. And it is here also that the fascinating concordances noted in d'Arcy Thomson's *Growth and Form* can be accounted for.

There is no possibility of transcribing such subliminal experiences into drawings or paintings without losing much, if not all, of their magic, for they are too soaked in their field-reference. But there can be no doubt that it is these primordial entities which lie at the roots of inspiration in the visual arts. No doubt equivalences of them also account for inspiration in poetry, music and in the other arts, as they also account for nature's own inspiration. It is the field which is tapped into in these subliminal meditations, shared by mind and nature.

Once this underlying creative flux has been felt in the scenes of nature, in its things and creatures, nature is seen in quite a different way; nothing is ever again merely a leaf, stone or insect, but the expression of some unseen but illuminating inspiration, fecund and profound. Then more correctly one can come to grasp the ceaselessly dynamic creative throbbing in nature, which has managed, in its finest moments, to create such wonder and abounding glory.

The influence of archetypes may determine the effectiveness, and human relevance of man-made things too. Landscape planning is probably at its best when it draws upon the relevant archetypes which have come into being in the natural design of landscape; those of rock formation, vegetative growth and ecological relationships. Buildings are also likely to draw upon the primordial archetypes involved in crystallisation as well as organic archetypes. Machinery is likely to owe its great symbolic powers to the fact that design and fabrication intuitively draw upon relevant inorganic and organic archetypes. In all probability, humans cannot make anything of significance or value which does not draw upon such protoforms, thereby gaining the advantages of a field involvement. There may thus be limits to the synthetic ability of mankind which are likely to limit his interference, for instance, in so-called genetic engineering.

CHAPTER 6

A human-centred Universe

Determinism in nature's evolution, accounting for its ever increasing interaction and guidance of archetypes, has so far omitted an essential, all-correlating principle. Without this, it is a fantastic and wonderful, but essentially meaningless enterprise. This principle is to be found in the culminating evolution of the nervous system and brain. The humanisation of the primate brain finally brings into being a creature aware of itself, and of the Universe. In the past, it has always seemed evident to human beings that they were in some way the very pinion of the Creation; for the amazing power of the mind does put the human being apart from all else, however humble the human may be. Science has thoroughly obliterated this belief in the significance of the human presence in nature, in a Universe seen as meaningless and accidental.

It is therefore heartening to find that science is now in the process of re-establishing the focalising importance of the human being in the work of Creation. Curiously enough, this restoration is not coming principally from branches of science which should be the most aware of wholeness and thematic qualities in nature. It is coming chiefly from astrophysicists. But there are some notable contributions being made by biologists, as in the writings of the scientist, J. Lovelock ('The quest for Gaia', *New Scientist* 6 Feb 1975) who mentions the many examples wherein one finds a close cooperation between different aspects of nature: between the inorganic and the organic, as well as between lower forms of life to facilitate the existence of higher forms. This indicates an integrated, coordinated, overall creative effort on the part of the planet to bring the human creature into being. In so doing, according to Lovelock, nature acquires the equivalent of a nervous system and brain of its own. Although Lovelock does not go so far as to state this explicitly, this can only make sense if the individual human mind can pool together with nature. This would happen automatically in the viewing of mind here proposed, for the mind has been defined as an organisation of the field by the brain. Although careful not to make such sweeping and revolutionary inferences, Lovelock does recognise that he is dealing with an extraordinary phenomenon with god-like attributes, for he revives an ancient Greek earth goddess, Gaia, as an apt name for this power.

This is a clear and forceful expression of a teasing idea which has been in the mind of scientists for a long time. Many chemists have been struck by the astounding congeniality of such elemental substances as water, as the carbon atom for life. Even a mechanistically-minded biologist like Crick, the co-discoverer of the structure of DNA, has admitted that the chances for life to arise from the non-living are astronomically remote. There has been a growing realisation among an ever increasing number of biologists, that some natural factor is missing from the present endeavour to reach a satisfactory understanding of life. Its field involvement is the most readily available explanation. Once this step is taken and the potential resources of the creative field realised, then it can begin to be seen that nature's self-found direction and theme leads naturally and inevitably to the human being: the unique possessor of the most evolved material structure in the Universe, the human brain.

Some astrophysicists have come to this conclusion by considering the very precise settings of the natural constants which control the togetherness of the atom and its reactivity. Computers have enabled equations to be worked out concerning the parameters within which the nuclear activities of stars could operate, following which planets could form, with the appropriate conditions, for the evolution of the enormously complex molecules on which life depends. It has been found that these parameters are extremely narrow. Had they differed by only a few percent either way, stars would either not have formed out of the swirling mists of hydrogen, or those that formed would have exploded or failed to start up their nuclear furnaces. Furthermore, the equations indicate that the life-compatibility of planets depends on a very exact setting of the nuclear constants. It is therefore apparent that the creation of matter, in its very special form in this Universe, is such that it would not only evolve, but that it would do so in a way that life, and in time, mind, came into being.

The British astrophysicists, Rees and Carr, have expressed this sensational conclusion in a new concept dependent on quantum theory: the Anthropic principle. This coincides with another wide-ranging inference in astrophysics, namely, the universality of planetary life, and its probable similarity with life on earth. It is now generally accepted that 'normal' stars like the sun, the most common in the Universe, are on average likely to spawn a planetary system; and on at least one or two planets in such systems, life-congenial conditions will occur. On some, life will be likely to evolve into human-like forms. A few decades ago, astrophysicists and astrobiologists concurred with science fiction writers that virtually endlessly different forms of life could arise elsewhere, due to the versatility of the carbon atom. But now that the extremely precise requirements of life and mind-making are better realised, it is accepted that life is indeed a very special achievement requiring very special conditions, and this is likely to be much the same everywhere.

Quite recently, Rees and Carr have focalised the Anthropic principle in the scale proportion of the human and the cosmos, from the atom to the entire Universe. They measured the proportion of objects in the Universe in reference to the size of a molecule and of a galaxy, multiplying the big and the small numbers together and taking the square root. This resulted in a magic number, indicating that the size of the earth is a geometric mean of the size of the Universe (which can be calculated from relativity theory) and the size of the atom. The mass of the human being is in turn a geometric mean of the planet and the mass of the proton. These proportions are further related to the electromagnetic and gravitational constants, which indicates that they are truly fundamental. We are left in no doubt that the Universe has been programmed to make us, because in some way we are necessary to the working of the Universe and its possible fulfilment.

The anthropologist, Gregory Bateson, concluded his search for meaning by stressing the necessity for the human mind to be seen as a functional aspect of nature (*Mind and Nature*; a necessary Unity, N.Y. 1977). This cannot make sense at all if the mind is conceived of as merely an aspect of the brain. However, as a field entity created by the living, experiencing brain, it is inevitable that mind and nature meet at the most fundamental of effective levels: the field. This means that the mind must in some way affect the fundamental working of nature. If some paranormal evidence is accepted, notably telekinesis, then one must suppose that the mind can influence the material world at its basic level of quarks and electrons, via the field. What could be the significance of this possibility in the evolution of Creation? What is the significance of human consciousness, so utterly inexplicable in ordinary material terms that it must imply the evolutionary elaboration of a very special field quality, exploited to its full power?

CHAPTER 7

The key relevance of consciousness

Professor J.A. Wheeler of Yale, a cosmologist of international status, has proposed what he calls a 'self-referent cosmology' as the best accounting for all the available evidence, especially for the evolution of matter into life, mind and consciousness. Although expressed in mathematical terms, for the ordinary non-mathematical person this simply means that the Universe begins as a universal, unorganised state and folds back upon itself, thanks to evolution, in a highly evolved, self-conscious form: a proposal which evidently accords with the Anthropic principle. This model is not easy to grasp, for in our ordinary existence everything has a beginning and an ending in clock time. Relativity theory teaches that more fundamentally, time is something very different. As a unity, the Universe could have no separated beginning and end. It can only possess distinct phases in a continuity of being, in terms of which Wheeler's self-referent cosmology makes mathematical sense. But this could only be properly grasped by a superior being able to see the process as a whole, or, more abstractly, by the mathematician.

Being a unified whole, what happens in apparently separated planets throughout the Universe must be basically unified. This cannot be at the material level, whereat distance is very real and the limitations of communication are set by Einstein's theory – the speed of light. It can only apply at the level of mind. Because of the universalising property of the field at such a level, the individual distinctiveness of mind, attached to a particular brain, may be thus sometimes overcome.

To common sense, this universalisation appears to entail a smothering of the mind's experiencing reality, the common sense rational mind being a sharp focalisation of consciousness serving a material existence. Other aspects of mind are not so focalised; on the contrary, they are expansive and all-embracing, as certain dreams indicate. If, as we have suggested, the field in its most evolved, organised state is the culminating product of evolution in matter, space and time, then this common sense impression is quite wrong. Far from being a smothering of the acuity of experiencing, the use of those aspects of mind most in contact with the field and least related to material life, amounts to an expansion. This intensifying of experiencing could turn consciousness into super-consciousness. This is not merely theoretical. There is a mass of evidence to show that minds do pool as in telepathic phenomena, and that high, peak participative states are a reality, touching into indescribable and ineffable categories of hyper-consciousness and hyper-experience.

Consciousness, as already implied, is best interpreted as a field potentiality which has been exploited and intensified by the evolution of the brain. Usually, consciousness is focussed on the material world, life and existence. But even so, it is subtly influenced by the emotional aspect of mind. This might be seen as partly a discreet field guidance, a view which is strongly verified in peak experiences or transceding glimpses of some order other than the material. In these moments we share in the universality of the field. As minds pool on a universal scale, the universalising aspects come to dominate consciousness, so that one can then say that the Universe itself has become conscious. The attainment of human consciousness can then be seen as an indispensable prelude to the consciousness of the Universe.

Possibly all aspects of mind functionally overlap and pool. For instance, in the 'low' aspects, the emotions of fear, panic or aggression show an evident tendency to spread between minds, dominating the behaviour of humans in the mass and in groups. But such poolings naturally tend to be ephemeral, for in depending on the lower, subhuman and prehuman aspects of the mind, they lack the essential criterion of the humanised aspects, namely, wholeness. And lacking this supreme quality, their pooling would tend soon to disassemble. They could therefore not contribute lastingly to a universalising consciousness. If only the most highly evolved, harmonious and whole can endure, it means that universal consciousness is necessarily humanly attuned. Here then, is the answer to the necessity of a humanised primate mind. The Universe could not have become conscious of itself without this prior achievement.

Such a cosmological achievement depends on the earlier mentioned Non-locality principle of quantum theory. From the start, this principle seemed to be implied in the theory, but it seemed so preposterous – from the traditional establishment viewing – that it was ignored. But even its possibility troubled Einstein. He devised the earlier mentioned experiment with the help of his colleagues, Rosen and Podolsky, to test this principle as well as other quantum properties which seemed absurd to him. It is only recently that techniques have become available to carry it out. But now Einstein's fears are confirmed. The Non-locality principle is true, as is the decisive impact of the human mind on quantum decisions in nature.

From our ordinary, common sense viewing of things this sounds utterly ridiculous. But taking into account what has been recently discovered about nature and cosmos, such principles are inevitable. Indeed, nature could not have operated in any other way if its operations were to be integrated, whole and relevant. It would have been tragic for human beings to have discovered such principles and to have found out that they did not participate in them and share in their universalising fulfilment. So the anthropic discoveries of the last decade have truly restored the pivotal human role in nature, and assured the individual of a meaningful place in the working of Creation.

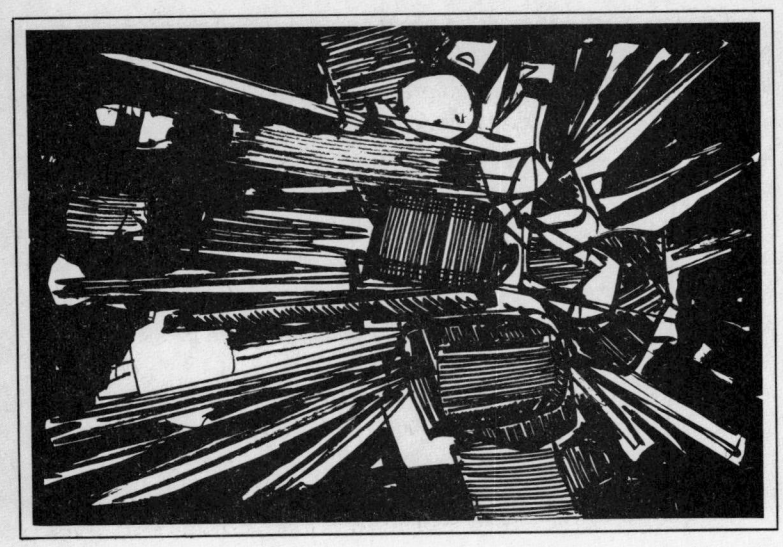

CHAPTER 8

The work of creation

In the light of these conclusions, matter makes sense, for it is the means whereby the functional Universe becomes organised and in time evolves to self-awareness. As yet there is no way of testing this paradigm experimentally. The evidence for it is circumstantial. But as the field is being extensively exploited in electronic and laser technologies, the way is being prepared for such an eventual testing. At present the field is being exploited in a transient way, and the field involvement is entirely dependent on energy-consuming devices. If the mechanisms stop functioning, the field involvement is annulled. In superconduction, however, in a device known as a Josephson junction, the field effect persists when the initiating current is turned off. It would seem therefore that the first steps in creating persistent field effects have been taken.

But success depends on discovering a means whereby a key property of the universal field can be exploited, a success notably achieved by the brain and mind. As purely physical systems have managed to exploit this property in less complex ways, notably in stars, there is hope that man-made mechanisms will also succeed in so doing.

Wholeness is the key aesthetic quality. There is no art work without it. In the design of machines, wholeness is also decisive. While a machine begins by being poorly integrated and unwhole, and therefore unaesthetic, the whole-seeking way in which the human mind works enables the designer and engineer to integrate the design of a machine to be both aesthetically appealing and efficient. But up to now, even the best of machines operate at the gross material level and are therefore subject to the inherent resistance of matter. Living machinery, as in nerve and brain, operates at the molecular level with subatomic connections into the field, thereby benefiting from field qualities such as wholeness.

An absolute efficiency could only be achieved by dispensing with material machines. Nature appears to have succeeded in doing just this. At the lowest energy level of an atom, there persists a basic vibration which does not consume ordinary energy – the energy which is available for all the other activities of matter. The apparently limitless energy of the field itself is used. Possibly living systems have found a way of exploiting such energies which necessarily escape the usual energy measurements, enabling life to defy the Second Law of thermodynamics – which every living creature apparently does by growing, creating, breeding, living. The Second Law of thermodynamics states that from its start, the Universe was supplied with a finite amount of energy, which ever since has become progressively less available – a process known as entropy. Entropy may be defied by nature's process of new energy pouring into the Universe from 'white holes' in the centre of nebulae.

Another indication that life makes use of the limitless energies of the field, is in the realisation of the aesthetic qualities which we have claimed to be field derived. The incorporation of such qualities in cells, tissues and organs, and in entire organisms, does not consume ordinary entropic energy. To make something beautiful need not consume more energy than to make it aesthetically neutral or ugly. Nonetheless, some form of energy is necessary to enable the field qualities to be made manifest in material things and creatures. The way this can be done is suggested in a recently-discovered natural phenomenon, quantum 'tunnelling', whereby a subatomic event, lacking the energy to achieve a particular transformation, can borrow from the limitless energies of the field. Necessarily such a borrowing has to be paid back or cancelled, but temporarily, the Second Law is broken. Life has almost certainly discovered the way of exploiting this loophole in natural law. It borrows field energy to make things beautiful, whole and harmonious, as it does to make them vital.

Such a borrowing can be annulled at any time, as when an animal dies. It is also immediately annulled as the usual energy needs of life are measured, for such a measuring interferes with the whole, integrated state of the organism. Thus the scientist cannot measure the field borrowing – a situation which accords with the now well-known quantum principle that the observer necessarily interferes in what is observed, at the fundamental levels of nature.

Nature accumulates and pools information and its playback into existence, with an overall control of phenomena. This points to a superintendent, overseer principle. The emergence of the radically new in evolution indicates that its field can process information for present and future needs in both physical and living realms. This can be done opportunistically, ignoring any overall theme, as in the efficient adaptation of shark or snake: creatures which can have nothing to do with the Anthropic principle. But over longer stretches of time the Anthropic influence is sensed and a theme is worked out. If the earlier stages of evolution appear to be random and blindly groping, the higher levels are visibly deterministic.

As always in nature there are many wasted efforts, but the theme gains ever-increasing authority; a conclusion which alone can explain the numerous startling instances of the most determined action in nature: as in the stubborn journeying of nerve fibres across the brain to their precise destination. In what really matters, nature shows a mind-shaking expertise.

Sexual reproduction has probably been devised to make this

field guidance all the more effective. The genes are strung along the chromosomes in cell nuclei. Prior to sexual reproduction the chromosomes are halved, otherwise every time the male and female chromosomes join the number of chromosomes would be doubled. This process is known as meiosis, and it provides the opportunity for quite extraordinary manipulations of genes and of entire chromosomes. Fragments of genes are broken off and rejoined elsewhere, so that quite new gene assemblies result. This cannot be blind and random. Indeed, those who once held that the mutations of genes occurring randomly could account for the new in evolution, have discovered that all such random gene changes are harmful and threaten the survival of the individual. Gene changes can only take place in an overall coordinated way, which is a situation defying a mechanical interpretation. It is essentially holistic. The only analogy is to be found in the overall interaction of particles in the quantum gauge field.

One of the most remarkable biological discoveries of recent years is the evidence that the organelles of the cell have evolved separately, as distinct primitive organisms subsequently assembled into the making of the cell in both plants and animals.

The cell organelles are the nucleus which controls the overall life of the cell, its reproduction etc. Other organelles consist of mitochondria: minute, folded, granular bodies, half a dozen or more in every cell, which deal with the cell's energy requirements, essentially thanks to a magical substance, adenine phosphate. Another organelle which some cells possess is the flagellum or the cilia. This is able to move substance to and from the vicinity of the cell by their swaying movements. What Margulis has discovered is that the mitochondria, the chloroplasts (in plants), as well as the flagellae and possibly other organelles, are in fact distinct microorganisms which can be bred separately when removed from cells. So at the dawn of life these different microorganisms evolved in very special ways and subsequently assembled – the assembly had to be instantaneous for the cell to work at all. There could be no clearer demonstration of an extremely canny supervision of the business of life and evolution.

This is so for interacting enzyme systems as well. As these

different components had to be assembled in one stroke for the earliest cells to function at all, a wand-like force clearly had to intervene, which only a field-involving paradigm can account for naturally. But other arresting examples in biology are legion, not only in the development of the embryo but also in the healing of a simple wound; in the most complex interrelationships of insect behaviour, in the prodigies of animal navigation, and in much else. In all such instances, chemical gradients and other physical controlling systems are clearly involved, but the overall direction cannot be traced to the physical level. It has to be initially superintendent.

CHAPTER 9

Evolution:
the field-directed theme

It is the suddenness of the creatively new in evolution which especially calls for an overall, transcendent supervision and coordination. The first cells are an example. Look at the quite astounding complexities of their division mechanisms and nucleation. The invention of such key molecules as chlorophyll, the design of the backbone, the provisions for flight, the coordination structures involved in vision and in hearing, all have left no intermediate fossils or stages. Compare this with the slower adaptative changes in which natural selection alone is an adequate explanation, and which progressive fossil records abundantly illustrate. The creative jumps of evolution can only be accounted for by a long accumulation of expertise in the field, resulting in creative decisions which are rapidly and effectively implemented in space and time.

It is only recently that this very special, saltational feature (Latin 'saltare', to jump) has been admitted, as the fossil evidence has been looked at more critically. All the major creative achievements have left a very poor succession of fossils or none at all. For instance, in the passage of life from the gill-breathing fish to the lung-breathing animals, there are virtually no succession of fossils. The very few creatures which have lung-like organs while living mostly in water, are generally accepted to be freaks: their organs not representing an actual transition. This paucity of fossils in the key creative events of evolution contrasts sharply with the very extensive successions of fossils in the rest of evolution. For evolution does consist largely of progressive change in which natural selection on neo-Darwinian lines is decisive.

Understandably, the evidence of saltation has caused a major commotion in biology as desperate attempts are made to remove this awkward evidence; for neo-Darwinism is only valid if a continuous progression of slow, minor changes applies. Saltation calls for a quite different method of evolutionary creation for which, I would suggest, only the field-involvement of life can account.

Because nature works so gropingly, a large diversity of created things and creatures is necessary, so that at least some will meet the Anthropic needs. So fantastic is this spawning of divergent creations that, superficially, it may seem random and without any underlying pattern. That this fecundity is nonetheless limited is indicated by the dominance of certain motifs — all flowers have a structural resemblance, as do birds, fish and mammals. But there are limitations to diversity as the higher forms are reached; there are millions of insect species, but only a few higher primates.

As matter can be formed in virtually endless ways. Carbon and silicon atoms offer billions of molecular configurations and DNA could code for millions of proteins different from those made use of by life — nature's creativity must be seen as limited rather than heedlessly profligate. The selection to meet the Anthropic needs is best conceived as occurring in the field. It is there that constraints must exist on the kinds of things and creatures which can in fact come into being. Where ever the Anthropic planetary conditions are met, much the same kinds of things and creatures — the same kinds of rocks and landscape as we know on earth, are to be expected. But variations within a theme are virtually unlimited.

Relativity theory has provided a good account of gravity, a non-material force responsible for all the astrophysical events in the 'curvature' of the space-time continuum. In so doing, what Newton referred to as a separate 'force of nature' disappears, becoming an intrinsic part of the fabric of Creation, and best understood as the first and most subtle influence of the direction of the universal field in matter, space and time. In spite of persistent attempts, no evidence has been found as to how gravity affects matter, for the effect is not material. 'Curvature' works via the field, and its directives, subtle as they are and requiring such immensities of time, are completely non-material.

But so far, relativity theory has failed to account for the expansion of the Universe. That too will have to be traced to a particularity of the field, insown at the very start of the Universe. The evolution of astral objects, nebulae and stars may be related to an interaction of gravity and expansion. But given the very precise and striking ways of evolution – both nebulae and stars began relatively inefficiently and got better at the job as field-experience accumulated – evolution, at the astronomical scale, is probably set off and controlled by inherent properties of the universal field. This is probably also true for the evolution of life.

The evidence that the field is involved is to be found in the ecological webbing of life, between living things and between life and environment; a process which has only relatively recently been fully appreciated. Formerly, the lack of a sufficient understanding of life allowed it to be seen disjointedly: as species existing independently and the relation with other creatures and the environment only judged superficially. The ecological webbing cannot be accounted for mechanically; it is very much a holistic, field property brought out into existence and exerting a very decisive influence.

Other striking evidence of the field is evolution's organisation into hierarchies, the first and most striking being the passage from the non-living to the living. Another is the passage from the vegetable to the animal, the former accumulating the sun's energies for the benefit of the latter. Others are the emergence of mind and emotionalism. Characteristic of such a staggered, hierarchical way of working is that in each new level quite new properties and qualities appear in no way derivable from the preceding level. Again, there is no mechanical explanation of this process. The essential differences between levels must be predetermined in the field, so that one comes to the conclusion, already hinted at, that the main stages of evolution in space and time have in fact been a part of the potentialities of the field, implemented by the archetypes. Evolution was bound to become thematic and teleological, in a Universe programmed to go a very particular way.

CHAPTER 10

The birth of emotion

Emotion is also a field quality which has been exploited by evolution. In most animals, the 'lower', bodily-connected emotions are so closely associated with physiological responses that they appear superficially to be a part of them. But in the apparent joy of certain animals, as in the frolics of the colourful creatures of a coral reef, in the fluttering of butterflies and in bird behaviour, a quality quite distinct from the physiological emerges. In such creatures, the experiencing of this quality seems to be immersive. There is no step back, no separate awareness of it. For this emotionalism to become conscious of itself it had to gain an independence from the neural machinery, and this has happened, as far as one can judge, only in the humanisation of the primate mind.

Accordingly, in the human genesis a jump occurred into a quite new level, marked by an extremely powerful emotional involvement, transfiguring all human experience and impregnating it with a profound human relevance. Even in ordinary existence this persists discreetly, ensuring that the human predisposition remains human.

A quality quite separate from the awareness of the material world had to be introduced, enabling a distinction to be made between the bare reflex awareness shared by all life, and a self-conscious feeling in respect of this awareness. To begin with this emotional component was necessarily immersive, more or less completely smothering the bare material awareness. But a sharpening of the distinction followed, providing the human with the ability to distinguish a material world at the same time that an emotionalised component assured the human that such a world was not hostile and meaningless, but humanly congenial. From then on a distinct emotionalised life of the mind became possible, the most distinctive human feature, and the most relevant to the Universe's eventual self-awareness.

Evolution first managed to achieve this transfiguration of experience by the emotionalisation of sex, long previously emotionalised in primate mother love, but persistingly opportunistic and unemotionalised in the primate male. The emotionalisation of mate bonding was indispensable for the long nurture of the human infant, made necessary by a slowly learning brain. A similar need had arisen in birds, for a different reason, accounting for the enduring mate bonding in many bird species.

So in the human, the emotionalisation of sex meant that the gratifications involved were no longer exclusively focussed on coitus, but on a sustained loving relationship, entailing sensitivity, altruism and mutual consideration. This humanising predisposition enforced a sensitivity to the beauty of the human face and form, to beauty and harmony in nature.

Although an emotionalised predisposition is the mark of the human, the emotional order is ignored in our matter-of-fact culture, because it cannot be precisely defined. As a quality of the field, exploited by nerve and brain, emotion can best be conceived as a kind of highly organised and versatile quivering, akin to the vibrations inherent in the field which we have found to be the likely origin of vitality. In being worked up by nerve and brain, this quivering becomes the creative 'substance' of the mind, providing its own imagery, its own world and life. When this is projected upon the outside world, the outside world becomes transfigured with emotional meaning. (see my *Art as Understanding*).

The outside world must be congenial for this projection to take place, a congeniality which explains how purely material things such as a mountain, the leaping tide, the majesty of clouds, can be seen as emotionally meaningful. Emotional life emphasises a potentiality inherent in all things. Without such an arrangement, it is quite unlikely that the peacock could have been made so emotionally enticing to the peahen, or that the human being could ever have come to love, to make music, to paint or write poems. Musical instruments are possible only because some materials, — including living tissues, — are made of atoms and molecules which resonate in a musical way. It is the field which ensures this interaction.

If, as we have already contended, the Creation is a functional enterprise, and the universal field the very basis of reality, then the emotional order can be understood as the ultimate creative resource. Matter is there only to make the emotional possible. It is the emotional which provides the measure of relevance in the Creation. It will be useful to keep this in mind, in the following attempt to arrive at a meaningful definition of the human.

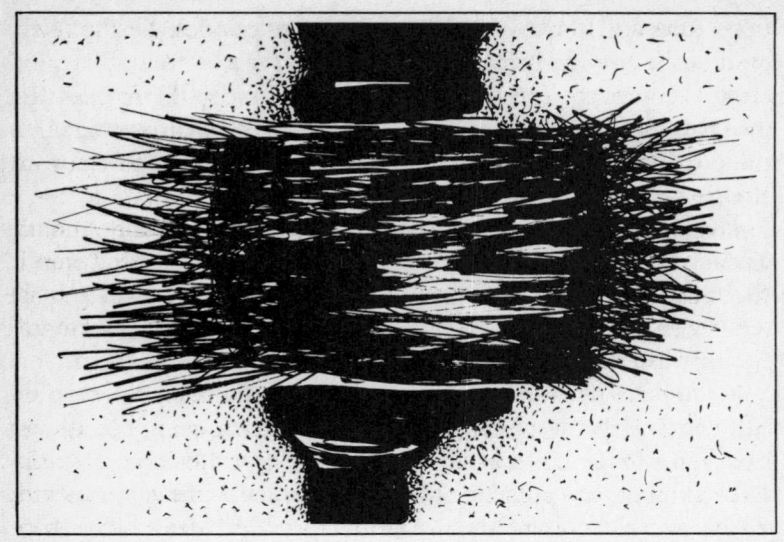

CHAPTER 11

Aesthetics and life

The aesthetisation of the human form is often concealed by the malformations of existence, notably by the deformations resulting from wrong eating, excess fat and from disease. But painters have always sensed that the human body, at its holistic best, is the very paragon of beauty in all of nature. The great masters of the Renaissance had no doubt about this at all.

This aesthetics is a matter of proportion. One recalls that Michelangelo and Leonardo, among others, felt strongly that the proportions of the limbs, trunk and head accord with some fundamental harmony in the way that the 'golden mean' expresses an ideal proportioning of the visual field. Others have also felt that there was a divine quality in this proportioning, traceable to the very roots of Creation. In more modern language, the astrophysicists, Rees and Carr, have reformulated this cosmological relationship of the human form, as earlier mentioned.

An important feature of this aesthetisation is the smoothness and hairlessness of the human form. This, the writer suggests, is due to neotony; the retaining of embryonic features in the adult. In the human case, neotony goes further, for the primate foetus is almost identical to the human foetus, free of hair and smooth-bodied. So some essential aesthetic steps may have been taken in the foetal primate before the advent of the human, although the adult ape lacks these features, becoming hairy, and its limb and body proportions altering.

An aesthetically-attuned, emotionalised predisposition is the most distinctive demarcation between man and ape, for as regards physiology man and ape are nearly identical. The ape may only have a rudimentary intellect, but it is there. But the ape's viewing of life is still reflex and not emotionalised, providing it with no standpoint to contemplate itself or the world distinct from itself. Such an achievement must have needed a very special nurturing environment: peaceful, beautiful and serene. A violent and ugly habitat could not have sponsored the work of humanisation – a point which has been missed by many contemporary anthropologists.

Bearing in mind the uncouth and unaesthetic conditions and creatures of the early earth, the planetary field must have solved enormous problems in climate, geology and biological habitat, to provide the favourable conditions necessary for humanisation. There is good evidence that this occurred relatively rapidly, in the Cretaceous, when colour harmonies first came into the world. The primate colour sense was first evolved to pick out fruits. Flowers subsequently provided the external stimulus for the further evolution of the exceptional human colour sensitivity, hundreds of different hues being distinguishable by the average person.

A richly floralised environment has thus been indispensable for humanisation, providing the mandalic forms of flowers. Their amazing colour symphonies, and their ecstatic scents, are the most potently humanising influences from the environment, and still so important in the higher moments of human existence. It is therefore to be expected that the floral refers to the most powerful of archetypes. But to produce a harmonious landscape with an integrated floral and vegetative contribution, with special rocks, soils, mountains, rivers and streams – qualities which landscape painters have so wonderfully extolled, must have called for sustained and expert field direction.

The Cretaceous was marked by a momentous geological event: the drifting apart of the continents and the setting in of the world climatic zones which have now returned after a temporary interruption by the Ice Ages. This feat of guidance has all the features of a unified and controlled creative act. It has played a decisive part in the origin and spread of flowers, in the rise of mountains and the creation of valley conditions, and provided the parameter of the earth we now inhabit.

Very special requirements had to be met, some of which had been solved in the primate emergence. A preponderantly fruitarian diet, typical of the higher primates, may have been needed to enable the brain and mind to evolve with the least metabolic disturbance. A predatory diet, or even a mixed one, would probably have provided too many mind-disturbing substances. High protein intake, is now known to have startling effects on mind, predisposition and behaviour.

Why the humanisation of the primate entailed an erect posture, remains officially unsolved. If this occurred well before the ice ages, as is now believed, it could not have been induced by a failure of the typical arboreal primate foods which abounded in the Miocene and early Pliocene. Adaptation to ground living does not demand an upright posture, as the baboon shows. It is not a change to be lightly considered, for it demands a very complex revolution in anatomy.

I suggest that it is a part of the aesthetic transfiguration of the human form and intimately connected with the change from an opportunist primate coitus to one embracing and adorative. In all other primates, indeed in all mammals and even in insects, copulation consists of the mounting of the female by the male. In the primates it also acquires a symbolic role – dominance by the male. Sexual love demanded a sharing of the act, a full awareness of the partner, hence the abandonment of the mounting posture for a face-to-face embrace. The revolution in anatomy which enabled an upright posture was another one of those feats of creativity which probably occurred with relative suddenness. The latest evidence is that the Australopithecines were not erect, and were anyway probably not on the human line. Only *Homo erectus* was suddenly and completely erect, with no intermediary stages so far found.

Having become an erect ground-living creature for reasons of love, and as a result, a poor climber, the earliest humans needed an abundance of low-growing fruits, and a substitute for the nuts which provide the primates with much of their protein. The abundance of grasses in the Miocene, the ancestors of cereals, met this need. Early man had no need of hunting.

CHAPTER 12

The dawn of Surreality

The highly exacting conditions necessary for humanisation mean that only on special planets are they likely to be met. Then, evolution is likely to proceed in a way very similar to that on earth, with much the same kind of landscape and creatures. So exacting is this process that unless the right conditions are met evolution does not get under way at all, as it has failed to do in the other planets of the solar system. A built-in tripping device ensures that the field impact of mind is not disrupted by contesting differences. This is of less importance at the lower stages of evolution, when diversity rules. But at the human level, standards have to be universal, if a universal pooling of compatible mind contributions is to provide the Universe with its self-awareness.

This universal pooling of human mind contributions results in a new level in the universal field with startling properties and powers. Such an achievement requires a special term. I have suggested Surreality, for this does bring into being an intensification of reality incomparably more powerful than the experiencing an individual mind can provide. Furthermore, Surrealism in the arts was first aware of this super reality in the dream and behind appearances. Some of its claims and practices have been confused, even absurd. But it does pinpoint, for the first time in human history, a critical awareness of a transcendental reality.

Surreality is made up of the quintessence of human experiencing: of other humans, of social existence, of the life of the mind and of nature in its widest definition. It embraces and heightens all that is beautiful, harmonious and joyful, reaching into the serene and glorious.

Like all new levels attained in the course of evolution, Surreality cannot be progressively entered into; it necessitates a jump from ordinary experiencing. This occurs in a special category of dreams which profoundly affect the entire predisposition on awakening. They are humanly enhancing and refreshing, although the contents of such dreams are often elusive. So powerfully humanising are such dreams, that they must have played an important part in the work of humanisation. This allows one to further infer that day time and night time were indispensable for an eventual humanisation.

Besides the dream, Surreality can be experienced in paroxysmal peaks of extreme intensity – the 'peak experience' as defined by the American psychologist, Abraham Maslow. Because of its strangeness, the study of the peak experience is still avoided by many other psychologists. The paroxysmal character of the peak experience is probably the consequence of the material preoccupations of civilisation. Among simple peoples, as among children, there is a more or less continuous dream-like participation, a state described by Lévy-Bruhl. Such a participation is qualitatively different from the civilised peak; it is immersive and oceanic, to the point that it impregnates the primitive's viewing of material reality with a dream-like content which, to the civilised, is judged to be distracting and confusing. In truth, it is potently humanising. Unless primitive man had been kept in such an all-transfiguring dream, he could not have faced the fearfullness of a distinct material world which the emergence of consciousness implied. It is this primitive condition, sustained in civilisations less materialistic than ours, which foreclosed the possibility of science arising. The materialism of high civilisation can thus be seen as a necessary trauma enabling a breakout from the primordial dream, and so tackling the challenge of a material world.

As the peak experience is a participative experience in Surreality, it transcends the ordinary timing of the clock. During the peak ordinary time is annulled and, as in the high dream, vast events can occur in seconds, exerting a subsequent influence for days or years. In focalising the surreal peak experience and in emphasising its distinctiveness, civilisation has simultaneously achieved a sharpening of self-awareness, the intellect and the material world. If, as is being suggested, reality is functional and the material world only necessary so that the functional aspects of the Universe can become organised, the apparent contradiction between intellect and intuition would seem to be self-defeating.

The sharpening of the intellect by civilisation and culture is indispensable, not only for an effective attention to the material world, but for a full and critical awareness of the challenge to transform the material by the inspiration of Surreality. Such an awareness is initially intuitive and not intellectual, and is best seen in the arts. In painting, for instance, the divine in the human, and the transfiguring of nature, are accentuated to the point that they can no longer be ignored. An intellectual awareness eventually emerges in philosophy and science, which should take into account the aesthetic involvement, a point so far not fully realised by philosophy and science. As a result of this fusion of intellect and high sensitivity a quite new awareness comes into being in civilisation. The present clash between intellect and intuition is misplaced, and one hopes it will be remedied by a science and philosophy of more wisdom.

Admittedly, in our present over-materialistic times, the peak experience is rare, and possibly some people are never aware of it. Or when it does occur, it tends to be dismissed as a lapse into impermissible fantasy. But conditions can be made more propitious for this experience, i.e. conditions more sensitising and humanising as it is encouraged by beauty, truth and harmony.

Sexual love probably consists of a sustained Surreal participation by both partners, the act of union thus occurring in Surreality and hence the perennial association of love and the dream. This means that although the bodily involvement is important, it is not predominant. This enables loving to pass to non-sexual forms: among the lovers themselves, in the family and in social altruism and compassion. These are the true resources of human communion and social cohesion. This also accounts for the fact that the most fulfilling love, sexual and non-sexual, is the kind which has a persisting quality, rather than being paroxysmal. True love can last, and as some have divined, can touch into eternity.

The peak experience probably dates back to the earliest civilisations. What is so striking about these is that they appeared with astounding suddenness, implying a forceful preparation in the field followed by a relatively rapid creative execution. The attainment of civilisation is thus part of the Universe's passage to self-awareness, involving the field and mind capable of participating in Surreality. A striking feature of such civilisations is not only their rapid development of skills in irrigation, metallurgy and in many other practical ways; it is their sharpened consciousness of themselves, of nature and of the Universe about them. This is attended by an awakened curiosity; a process coinciding with the Universe's own approach to self-awareness.

Humanisation has thus consisted of two stages: a preliminary dream-like protective immersion, possibly attained between one and two million years ago by *Homo erectus*; and a jump into a sharpened consciousness. This is not only of self, nature and cosmos, but of Surreality, which coincided with the attainment of civilisation. For over a million years this achievement, decisive to the Creation, was prepared for in terms of the field. The attainment of Surreality by the Universe therefore depends on the attainment of civilisation throughout the Universe. According to the Anthropic equations, the time needed for the emergence of life and mind coincides approximately with the present. In other words, we are likely to be among the first planetary systems to reach a life and mind-making capacity.

The first stage of surreal, dream-like existence only applied when the conditions of existence were humanly congenial. In glacial times, an aroused subconscious threatened this harmony, ushering in the low magical mind – magical rites endeavouring to placate the aroused demons. Low magic and witchcraft have dominated primitive existence, from the earliest humans of a million or more years ago to the rise of civilisation. But the magical mind has persisted, with rare interludes of a more humanly sensitive predisposition. To break the hold of magic, civilisation had to discover the therapy of reason first achieved in ancient Greece.

The contemporary mind has resorted to mind-enhancing drugs. However, the only real alleviation of this problem is a restoration of a belief in the meaningfulness of existence, and a more human world.

Mystical experience provides useful data regarding Surreality but it has tended to be an isolating, community-excluding and a world-evading pursuit, and as such, it is outside the trend of civilisation. But it has to be taken seriously. For in the thwarting conditions on this planet, there may well be no other way of attaining to the further reaches of Surreality. The obstacles encountered in this pursuit, in the so-called 'dark night of the soul', testify to the ferocity of the barriers to such high states of being.

Even in more favourable conditions, difficulties may persist in attaining the full peak experience. Possibly such difficulties are in fact inbuilt: a part of nature's strategy to prevent a neglect of material life which would result if the high reaches were too easily accessible. So at the best of times the peak experiencing of Surreality may never be at its fullest, but variously attenuated. Probably only following the complete stilling of the body and brain is an unstinted participation in Surreality possible. Most people do have some peak experiences, bringing sufficient refreshment to quieten the anxieties of existence. Young people in particular are often aware of a transfiguring hyperreality, especially in first love.

The work of painters and others in the visual arts, provide glimpses of the 'content' of Surreality, necessarily in symbolic ways.

Music touches into its rhythmic, harmonic qualities – the flux and flow of Surreal experiencing, whilst poetry weaves these attributes into the pulse of existence. Figurative painting, at its best and most accomplished in civilisation, shows how the opacity of material substance is transcended by light and colour, giving to recognisable forms and scenes the shimmer of Surreality.

Impressionism illustrates an intensification of the symbolic content which passes into the totally abstract, demonstrating the passage from figuration to the Surreal and functional springs beyond form and appearance. Expressionism marks the intrusion of the existentially aroused subconscious, anguished and menacing, but eliciting reactions of hypervitality in asserting forms, colours and textures. Equivalents of these great categories of Surreal revelation can be found in all the arts.

The disembodiment of experience in these is strongly contested by the intellect, which can only properly experience in an embodied context. But, it is contended (see earlier chapter), the quick of all human experiencing is its emotional component. As the emotional can only be expressed symbolically, then such a material disembodiment amounts to an accentuation of experiencing. Music and abstract painting demonstrate that superficial form is substituted by profound symbolic supports, so that content, far from being diminished, is actually increased. This is one resolution of a debate between the literal and the symbolic in the arts.

CHAPTER 13

Creation and sex

The advent of Surreality transforms the nature of the Universe. Not only does the Universe acquire an organ of self-awareness, becoming aware of itself and of its creatures, it also becomes capable of guiding and aiding the culminating stages of evolution, so that these are attained more perfectly and more speedily. This increasing spiral in evolution is apparent in the achievement of the human being, so speedily and effectively created that the species appears quite suddenly, fully formed. Surreality, in its furthest possible evolution, thus brings the Universe to its fulfilment. It is becoming a god-like focalising influence made in the image of the best in human beings. Such a god-like emergent force in the Universe must care and love the human being, and all that aids its advance.

To avoid the embroilments of theology, such an emergent Deity 'made by the Universe', now requires a special name. I suggest Theos. It is surely the same as that found in the revelation of certain mystics. The full attainment of such a power will probably transform the Universe, even in its material aspects, and some of the ordinary laws of physics will be superceded. As this has not happened, one must assume that the Theos is still emergent. But here and now, it is a force to be reckoned with in human existence, requiring human help and participation for its fulfilment. The Theos is the means whereby the disunity of the Creation is resolved in a culminating fulfilling love. To grasp this, it is necessary to trace the natural history of nature's divisioning and reunification through sexuality.

Nature, faced with the resistance of matter, divides. We see this in the separate evolution of cell organelles, in the separation of living matter into cells and in the separation of the sexes. Human sexuality brings this achievement to its full. An understanding of the role of sexuality is thus of cosmological importance.

The capacity for reproduction is inherent in the organisation of the DNA molecule, the zip-like parting of the two counter-spirals ensuring an identical recreation of the gene organisation. This is a mechanical facility, and if the creation of life was only an endless repetition of similar entities, it would have sufficed. But more creative change was required. Neither purely random gene change nor natural selection could do this. The latter accounts admirably for adaptation to change and for much of evolution, but it cannot account for the genuinely new and creative. At present, there is no explanation of this, which again is why a superintendent field aspect has to be called in.

The drive to reproduction emanating in the field takes two directions: one, separate and the other, unitive. Both are illustrated in the researches of the American biologist, Margulis, who has demonstrated that the organelles in all living cells are in fact primitive microorganisms which were captured by the earliest cells to form some three thousand million years ago.

These organelles, such as mitochondria, chloroplasts, and flagellae, have retained the ability to reproduce themselves independently of the cells they have helped to form and sustain. As the earliest cells could not have managed without these originally independent microorganisms, one is faced here with a stupendous act of assembly. This surely points clearly to a superintendent force.

These two counter working drives account for the origin of sex, and the separation into different non-sexual and sexual generations. In the bryophytes, in the fungi and algae, one encounters a very complicated dispersion of creative effort. Different kinds of non-sexual reproduction in one generation are followed by sexual activities in another, enabling wide variations in lifestyle, and therefore wideranging adaptability.

But with rising complexity the process became increasingly specialised into two categories: male and female. Even in bacteria, at a scale of 1/100mm, a male-like attribute, resembling a phallus, appears in certain individuals and is able to inject their DNA material into other individuals, acting as females. It is in this way that primitive organisms manage to defeat the ingenuity of bacteriologists who devise chemicals to destroy them. Those with better aptitudes for neutralising such poisons pass on some of their cell substance to their fellows, thanks to the transposon. In such a proto-sexual way, a particular species of bacteria can become resistant to a particular drug, such as penicillin. This phenomenon well illustrates the advantage of mixing separately acquired qualities and experience – the basis of sex.

This creative principle of dispersing, followed by reassembly or reunion, has also been used in other ways, e.g. in the metamorphosis of insects, which recalls the alternating sexual and non-sexual generations already mentioned. Such a fantastic creature as the butterfly could not be created in one go. The creative effort had to be spread out, specialised, and finally reunited in sex. The creative passage from egg, to caterpillar, to chrysalis, to adult sexually-mature butterfly is a feat of diversified creativity quite inexplicable in the one-level viewing of science.

The separation into two sexes means the establishment of different ways of life and experiencing in male and female. By combining these differences in the sexual act, a wealth of diversified experience is possible beyond the scope of a uniform non-sexual arrangement. The difference between male and female can very generally be described as expressive and receptive, with endless possibilities of variation from the molecular to the behavioural.

The early manifestations of sex in bacteria and the protozoa indicate a considerable sexual adaptability. Any bacterium can develop a transposon, and any one can serve as receptor to the transposon's sharing out of living material. Similarly, any two of the protozoan, euglena or paramoecium, can come together and exchange their cell contents. Although visible sexual demarcation into male and female is later important, even the higher animals retain a certain sexual instability, as is seen in the hermaphroditism of molluscs and in the sex changes of fish. Even in mammals and humans, the male retains certain female characteristics and vice versa. This indicates that sexual demarcation is not the aim, but rather the vehicle of qualities which transcend the mechanisms involved.

Sex is not only the means of blending separately evolved qualities in male and female. It is preeminently the means of creating quite new qualities. How ingeniously nature has arranged for this to be done has only recently become resolved. For the sex cells of male and female to be united, as already stated, their chromosome number has to be halved, otherwise the chromosomes, which contain the genes, would be doubled at every mating. This phenomenon of cell division, meiosis (mitosis is ordinary cell division, without a halving of the chromosomes) provides the startling opportunity to shuffle the genes around from one chromosome to another. At times, entire pieces of chromosome can be disassembled and reassembled. When one takes into account the fact that a random, unorganised change in a single gene is invariably disturbing, and at times fatal to the organism involved, one must be amazed that nature can manage such vast gene changes or mutations without disastrous consequences. In other words, nature mutates in a thoroughly integrated, holistic manner, which once again suggests a field superintendence.

It is thanks to this opportunity offered by the preparation of the sex cells in meiosis, that the field guidance of life can be implemented, and, as we have seen in the course of evolution, at times with staggering rapidity and efficiency. The biologist, Barbara

Maclintock, won the Nobel prize for observing an even further extension of this creative process: the actual jumping of genes from one chromosome to another at some far site in the nucleus of the cell, at just the right place to enable a fundamental change in the life response of the organism. Here is the field guidance of life making itself immediately visible at the microscopic level. The long pilgrimage of sexual evolution, from the humble yet most ingenious invention of the bacterial transposon to the mating of mammals and humans, can be seen as nature's inspired creative strategy.

Some other creative aspects of sex can be mentioned. Like only breeds with like. At the DNA level, only similar genes in male and female will pair along the chromosomes to form the normal chromosome number. Molecular incompatibilities are no doubt implied. But at the living, bodily level, an attraction for oppositely sexed members of a particular species, is sometimes accompanied by aversion or blockage to other species, even fairly closely related. This implies a more fundamental force. A predisposition of the nervous system is at work, initially reflex in the lower organisms but emotionalised in higher animals.

If the phenomenon, even in the simpler organisms, is seen as a pre-emotional involvement in sex, of like and dislike, then the field can be usefully brought in. This further suggests that the formation of different species is the consequence of predispositions invested in the field. Whether or not the full number of creatures is realised, depends on environmental and geological conditions. But given congenial conditions, the different kinds of creatures are limited by some sort of transcendental predisposition in Creation.

This accounts for the rigid separation of species, with no overlapping. If some such force had not been at work it is not possible to understand how different, yet related, species could have come into being. The first new members of a new species would surely breed back with the pre-existing species from which they have arisen; an old biological quandry which the field involvement thus solves.

Except possibly in the lowest microorganisms, sexual union is invariably subject to certain tests of vigour, which is logically understandable. Life would have degenerated very early if the unfit had been allowed to breed with equal ease with the fit. This testing is primarily physiological; a test of strength and endurance, e.g. in the fights for hareem creation in deer, and in the vortical nuptial flights of Mayflies. But with the emergence of an emotional involvement in sex, notably in some fishes, birds and in the human, emotional criteria gain importance.

A partial failure in the protection of the cell functions at the molecular level, might account for the genesis of the pathogenic viruses, which, with increasing knowledge, do appear to be genes gone wrong. A mind-shaking example of the ability of the sex cells to repair such possible damage to the molecular sex system is seen in the recent discovery that special enzymes are able to remove damaged portions of chromosomes, and replace them with new strips. They extirpate individual faulty genes followed by a healthy replacement. This feat quite clearly calls for a very precise and expert field guidance. Nature has gone out of its way to protect the 'germ plasm': the sacred continuity of sex-involved protoplasm transmitted in a continuous stream from the first living creatures to the present day. But things can occasionally go wrong, probably most often, if not always, due to some unusual or abnormal disturbance in body or environment.

The sex drive is such a compulsive force that it points to some supreme transcendent influence, an aspect of the field's 'pregeometry', an all-surmounting drive to be observed in the blind, frantic copulatory momentum of all creatures. By the time the higher organisms came along, this drive had become an even more powerful influence which one can best express as an influencing archetype. Animal, and indeed human behaviour, indicates that once this archetype is tapped into, the outfolding influence is truly obsessive and compulsive. The copulatory act runs on blindly into orgasm and fertilisation.

One can understand how difficult it has been for nature to curb and contain this compulsive drive in humanisation, having recourse to the field-involving, high humanising emotions in order to do so. And also how easily this curbing can be overcome by a revival of its primal power. The compulsive, autonomous field linked to the power of the sex drive means that it can be creatively diverted for uses other than sex. As Freud discovered, distracted from its sexual expression, it becomes the essential drive to cultural evolution and civilisation. Jung traced its creative power in every aspect of the psyche. That sex is a field-involving phenomenon accounts for its intimate involvement in the evolution of the nervous system, brain and mind, whose emergent features – feeling, emotion and consciousness – we have traced to an exploitation of the field.

Besides the compulsive sex drive, the gratification of sex is also to be seen as field-involving and pre-emotional, even in its most elemental guise in microorganisms. Its emergent 'receptive' and 'expressive' forms culminate in the male orgasm and in its qualitatively different but related climax in the female. The compulsive, ecstatic quality in this gratification is the basis of a field-unitive experiencing.

One can wonder why nature has had recourse to such complex, devious and dangerous ways of creation. Evolution remained ignored until recently, and sex, especially in its culminating human manifestation, remains largely misunderstood. The answer can only be that nature had no other alternatives. The extremely weak 'pregeometry' of the field could only be exploited by the contorted and laboured passage of evolution, and by the strange antics of sex and reproduction.

It is evident that this fantastic way of creation can make no sense if the goal is only in elaborate sexual mechanism and behaviour. Sense is only possible if sex, as much as evolution, has all along been striving for a programmed development of traits and acquisitions which transcend the physiological, biological and cerebral mechanisms involved. In other words sex, like evolution, serves some profound cosmological destiny, for which matter and body have been indispensable, but which is not to be found in the material order. Science has proclaimed, from its limited and inadequate viewing, that sex and evolution appear random and meaningless. It is only when judged from the highest level of their development, at the human level, that they make sense, as I shall attempt to show.

The orgasm, previously an essentially male prerogative, became intensely emotionalised and something like it, but qualitatively very different, is experienced by women. In both male and female, while the climax focalised the ecstatic joy of loving, sexual love acquired a time-transcending quality because of its involvement in Surreality. This lasting effect was easier for nature to achieve in the woman than in the man, for the female mammal had known enduring mother love for millions of years. But even in the human male, with his long opportunist precedent, sexual love can be intensely humanising. Lovers do acquire something of the divine; of the Surreal.

CHAPTER 14

Love and time

Occurring in the purely functional millieu of Surreality, transcending space and time, union does not consist of an exchange of parts. One can truly love the whole of nature, the whole of Creation; and it is in such all-embracing love that cosmological fulfilment must lie.

In ordinary existence, with the sexual differences dominating, it is not easy to grasp such a process. But even then, an equalising tendency can be seen to be at work: the woman becoming more assertively self-aware and free from her ancient hormonal bondage, and the man more feminised and sensitive. This unification, surmounting the overt demarcations of sex, has long been realised to be an essential condition for the attainment of the higher reaches of mind. In alchemy it has been expressed as the 'divine marriage' leading to the androgyne: a unified state which abolishes all the separations and disunities.

Human sexuality has been discussed in some detail as it is the essential premise to an understanding of the Theos, and its relation to the higher reaches of love and ecstatic joy. The revelations of mystics have been frequently expressed in a language ripe in sexual nuances. But it should be seen as sex in a transfigured Surreal sense, having nothing in common with lust. Unfortunately no words exist to describe, even symbolically, such categories of experience and so words which apply to lower stages in the evolution of the process have to be used.

The Theos brings the evolution of love to its uttermost fulfilment, vanquishing all separation, and provides at its purest the rapture only intimated in the orgasm. Properly understood, the orgasm, is a prelude to divine love. The Theos is all love, all joy. The sexualisation of the Deity, which has occurred throughout human history, refers to lower levels in the emergence of the theotic process, just as polytheism represents an initial primitive dispersion of its powers. The masculine godhead has adapted to patriarchal situations. The human psyche cannot be sane and whole without these symbolised contacts with the Theos.

Loving the Theos is the assurance that death can be vanquished. The cosmological need for loving on which the fulfilment of the Universe depends, could well be the explanation of death. It should be possible to design a Universe in which death does not occur, for timelessness is inherent in the field, and even computer designers hope to construct perpetual self-repairing machines. But if such immortal creatures failed to love, the Universe's fulfilment would be frustrated. So those who cannot love, must die.

Human loving is the natural initiation to the love of the Theos. Indeed all loving, of nature and of its creatures, should be appreciated as a means of initiation, and is probably indispensable to theotic union which alone guarantees that the human being can transcend time.

In the pre-scientific stages of civilisation it seemed reasonable that there should have been a Creator God of the Universe. Science has eliminated the need for such a contradictory concept. The

Universe, in every aspect examined, indicates its permanent self-consistency. The notion that a Deity could have emerged into being as evolution proceeded was proposed in the twenties by the mathematician, Samuel Alexander, who suggested that space-time was capable of bringing it into being. It will be recalled that in relativity theory, space-time is a mathematical device which deals with the emergence of space, time and matter out of the continuum or universal field. Alexander was therefore correct in assuming that space-time possessed strange and powerful creative possibilities. But without a 'pregeometry', an Anthropic principle and without a material world programmed to organise the field, an intra-cosmic Godhead is impossible. Alexander's Deity was limited and unsatisfactory.

The concept of the Theos, as well as the possibility of a persisting human participation in Surreality, depends on a satisfactory understanding of time. 'Pregeometry', and its aesthetic loading, is timeless. But as the field is organised by material events, a variable timing of the persistence of such assembled field entities becomes possible. When they share in the field's wholeness they are timeless or eternal, as judged by the clock in our experience of the material world. As their intensity of functioning varies, so a variable experiential 'timing' of field events takes over. This variable experiential timing is encountered in dreams, under the influence of drugs, in the peak experience and in certain mental pathologies, such as schizophrenia. This variability of experiential time provides Surreality with its 'living time'.

As field events impinge into the material world, so they can be timed relatively by the clock. This depends on their degree of field involvement, which explains the clock paradox in relativity theory. In the life of the mind, there can be a similar relativity of timing. The more bodily and materially connected the events, the more claiming becomes the metronomic timing of the clock. It is also possible for a field-dependent experiencing to be judged as 'timeless' or 'eternal' from the standpoint of ordinary existence, and yet to possess its own 'timing', which would be the situation in Surreality.

Although Theos and Surreality are primarily concerned with

the high humanised aspects of the mind, Creation cannot be completely unconcerned with the lower. If the lower predominated, cluttering the universal field with deviancy, Surreality would be threatened. So one can expect that even in our alienated condition on this planet, supernal aid is likely to be forthcoming. Possibly the great messianic wave, covering a period of about a thousand years, can be accounted for as such a process of aid from the universal field with its transcendental ecology of staggering complexity and resource. The present culmination of materialism may have temporarily blocked such aid, but any recovery is likely to attract it once again, and possibly with greater effect.

CHAPTER 15

Prospects of immortality

For the human mind to fulfil its role in the work of Creation, its higher humanised aspects must transcend space and time in an enduring way. Transiency would undo the Universe's self-awareness. The possibility of such a continuity of experiencing beyond space and time, following the death of body and brain, is generally doubted today. For in a material viewing of reality, no possible 'environment' can be imagined as existing in which the disembodied mind could persist. Nonetheless, continuity is implied in the constitution of matter, for the field entities once formed by a material event share in the timelessness of the field. It is the assembled entities which can dis-assemble into incoherence. For the field assemblies to persist a suitable 'environment' is indispensable, as is their thorough integration and wholeness. Surreality provides such an environment, and a humanised existence supplies the enwholing feedback. Unwhole, inhuman minds incapable of loving, disintegrate in the midst of existence.

Surreality cannot be proved intellectually; it can only be experienced. But its reality does appear to follow from a functional viewing of mind, which the new physics makes possible. In this viewing the activity of a material brain is capable of generating events in the field which, once generated, exist in their own right, whilst depending on the brain for their expression and communication. From such a basis, in the new cosmology, the emergence of Surreality would appear to follow naturally. But officially, mind is not recognised as a separate reality. Workers on the brain still hope, in spite of a half century of complete failure, to find the characteristics of mind in some way attributable to molecular events. Of course such molecular events are involved in mind making, but the distinctiveness of mind refuses to be so reduced. So in desperation, philosophers like Ryle announce that there is no mind.

The subject is bedevilled by the fact that the most commonly observed aspects of the mind, reason and intellect, can be mechanically accounted for, as it is little more than a computing ability. An extremely complex neural organisation is surely necessary, but it is not the only requirement. Birds, with only a few grams of brain matter, have an intense emotional life, and whales and elephants have brains larger than humans, with neither comparable emotionalism nor intelligence. In fact, the quite sudden enormous increase in the human brain, which occurred around a hundred thousand years ago, may be an abnormality brought about by the very demanding material conditions of the Ice Ages. The great difficulties of human birth support this.

The right lobe of the brain is the most concerned with humanisation and the left, the most literal and materialistic. Possibly we have also overdeveloped our left brain, at least in Western civilisation. But judging from the extent of the *corpus callosum*, connecting the two brains, nature has made ample provision for an integrated functioning. It is up to us to find more whole and loving ways of life.

A concept in new physics which has a bearing on the interpretation of mind is the field concept. This provides the basis for a transcendental aspect in nature, its close functional relationship with the material order, and the ground of reconciliation between brain and mind. Another concept is the Non-locality principle, which makes telepathy inevitable. Another is the influence of 'the observer on the observed', which provides for the creative intervention of the mind in nature, the 'many worlds' interpretation of quantum theory, and the relativity of time.

The extreme focalisation of consciousness on the material world makes it very difficult to accept the possibility of more expansive forms of consciousness, as in dreams, love, the arts, and in drug-induced states. The new Gauge field theories in quantum physics provide analogies of an expansive, diversified and yet integrated category of activity, typical of the field. Field theories also provide analogies, admittedly simplistic compared with the complexities of mind, whereby 'things' and 'creatures', and so entire 'worlds' of experience with endless qualities, can arise out of the field. The material world is one particular direction taken by this process. The elaboration of the mind, transcending matter, is another.

It is the creative capacity of the mind which is the most startling, for usually the mind seems to be a fairly passive influence in nature. But there is sufficient evidence that in certain conditions even the limited human mind can achieve near miraculous feats. The new physics provides the ground in which such power can reside. A power no doubt invested in the field as a potentiality, but needing the vast edifice and pilgrimage of material evolution into brain to realise.

Participating in Surreality, the psyche, no longer focalised but expansive, acquires miraculous powers which are able to use Surreality to bring into being infinite realities. In this Creation, love is the ruling instrument, so that what is loved, happens. One has hints of this fantastic phenomenon in certain dreams, when persons and scenes known in life become transfigured. In ordinary existence, the individual appears to be quite isolated from others and from the environment. But this is so only regarding bodily experience. The psyche is participative and its transcendent function is ruled by love. All psyches participating in Surreality are necessarily united. So that what a psyche desires actually happens. Other psyches, other creatures and their accompanying scenes and content, are thus creative foci in a whole situation. Thanks to the human psyche's privileged situation in Surreality, all that is wanted can not only be realised, but acquires a timeless hyper-reality.

Comparison with linear experiencing of rational existence is extremely limited. For psyches sharing in Surreality, as in a post-mortal state, there would be no problem. What one wants, and what is wanted of one by others, would happen. Obviously a problem would arise as regards the relationship of living individuals, and that between the living and the dead.

But even in an apparently isolated existence, one is made constantly aware of a sustained communication between affectively related persons, which ignores space and time. Reunions after long separation are as if time had not mattered at all. And apart from this timeless togetherness in life, one often feels constantly sustained and guided by unknown loved ones.

Every creative writer is aware, at some time or other, of being taken over by the characters, scenes and places at first perhaps only tentatively imagined, as in a play by Pirandello. As the work takes form, so these characters gain autonomy and authority, becoming real and powerful influences on the work, often to the shock and consternation of the writer. Writers can ill afford to be mystics and seers. They have to keep a firm control, maintaining a strong relationship with the material world, with life. The mind does have virtually miraculous powers of creation in terms of the field, drawing upon resources beyond the ordinary. Once these things, these characters, have been sufficiently created, they can influence the outcome of the work, protesting at turns of events they disagree with, and even sabotaging the continuity of the work.

If this is so, the mere act of thought entails an enormous cosmic responsibility, for things created with sufficient verve and faith may well endure in a time-transcending sense, bringing into being new worlds of fantastic or fearful splendour. Some have thought that this is how we have come into being. This phenomenon provides clues of great interest concerning the possible destiny of the psyche after death. But apart from this well-nigh miraculous creative power of the psyche, one is surrounded by a vast and possibly unlimited constellation of beings, some related to known and loved ones, but others quite unknown in one's ordinary life. Loneliness is a materialistic fallacy.

It is certain that the linear concept of the psyche, that of common sense, is defective. People united by love, even in the midst of a distracting material existence, acquire a considerable degree of time-transcendency, feeling strongly that time 'does not matter'. In dreams, there is evidence that this manifold experiencing of the psyche takes place when several dreams occur simultaneously, running one into the other.

Postmortal continuity is beyond analysis or description. Evidence for it is inferential, essentially from the peak experience and from the basic qualities of reality in the new physics. There one finds just those properties which, while different from the common properties of the material world, provide the grounds for a belief in the transcendence of time. Up to now, the new physics has not concerned itself with the organisation of the field by material evolution. Therefore it can provide no indications as to how a transcendental environment, indispensable for any possible continuity, can be naturally provided. This is for the future, but here and now, can the possibility of postmortal existence be accepted as feasible?

The necessarily inadequate language used in attempts to communicate the peak experience are also likely to apply to postmortal continuity in terms such as beauty, ecstasy, joy, harmony, radiancy, illumination, spectral, musical, floral etc. Vitality is, as already suggested, a field property exploited by biomolecular systems. The same field potentiality is probably exploited in the making of Surreality, free of its physiological burden. States described as 'astral bodies', and transfigurations in music and art, may be visions of the Surreal.

The relationship between the living and the dead can be expressed in an analogy of Gauge theory. This is so important in the new physics, for it is the mathematical means of dealing with quarks; the gauge being a mathematical device which enables the entities in a field situation to be imminently coordinated. It can thus be understood as a move towards a mathematical holism. The psyche acts as a gauge, so that while identity is preserved, there is also an instantaneous and timeless codependence on all other entities present. This integration can be universalising.

In life, the gauge situation is highly restricted to enable the psyche to deal with an anti-gauge situation – material life, so that other gauge aspects are played down or obscured. Following death, there is an immediate shift in the gauge situation. Communication between the living and the dead, especially in a materially accentuating situation, is obscured, although it persists at higher levels. The need for this is obvious. For if there were no constraints in the gauge field of the mind on both the living, and between the living and the dead, material life would be disdained.

But in ordinary life communication can occur as the constraints are circumvented. It is naturally circumvented in primitives and children, which accounts for the communication with the dead in all primitive societies – the situation in human existence for over a million years. Civilisation has accentuated the constraints. But one can expect that in the future, when the material problem has been solved, such a communication will be restored. We happen to be in an awkward transitory situation.

One can conclude that the belief (as ancient as human kind) that the apparent finality of time is vanquished owing to the way in which matter, space and time have been set, depends on the fulfilment of the humanising conditions governing the mind. Reincarnation is the ancient belief that a particular psyche returns via another brain and body into this world. Like prediction, there is likely to be a confusion due to an intuited potentiality not realisable in the misguided form in which it has been usually expressed. Such beliefs are only possible by ignoring nature's working. But if by reincarnation one means a succession of 'worlds' and 'lives' in the transcendental destiny of the psyche, then some sense can be made of it. For nature does work in hierarchical jumps, each level forming a different 'world'. So this principle may well apply in the field worlds also, the psyche being 'born', 'living' and 'dying' in succeeding levels until Surreality is attained.

As for the evidence often claimed in support of reincarnation in the traditional definition of the subject, it is best explained as the parasitisation of living minds by fragments of disassembled minds and by psychic detritus of other lives. This is a well-attested phenomenon in the archives of the Society for Psychical Research which can at times result in complete possession.

Death can be a terrible agony of body and mind, an agony which could have an adverse effect on the destiny of the postmortal psyche. If the high aspects have been insufficiently consolidated during existence, this disassembly of the mind, as the cohering order of material consciousness is lost, might well disrupt the mind altogether. The menace of hell and damnation, which the modern age assumes it has managed to dismiss, may be a terrifying reality. One can observe the agony of disintegration in the insane. Help can possibly be given by love and caring, and by the use of drugs in the terminal alleviation of distress. But the only reliable assurance is a life lived wholly and humanly.

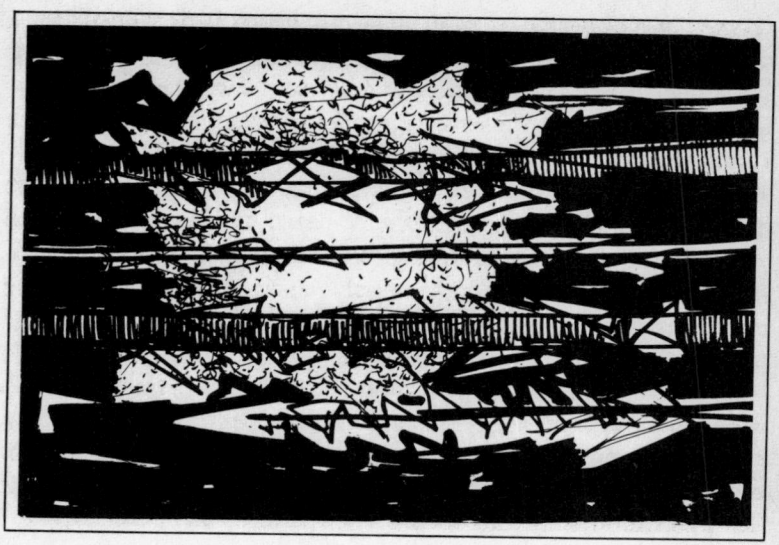

CHAPTER 16

The mind-determined future

In intuitively sensing such a possible human defiance of time, various beliefs have been entertained regarding the fate of the psyche: its relation to life, brain and body and to the past and future. Because of the hold of the material world, even in religious and metaphysical domains, any possible destiny in existence has tended to involve the material order, in presuming that the outfolding of material and vital events in the future is preordained, and therefore predictable.

The suggestion already made, of the way in which the mind is able to interact with the material brain – because the mind is an organisation of the field by the brain – is by no means the whole story. For Wheeler, Wigner and some other physicists, the mind acts upon matter not only via the brain, but in a far more fundamental way. Nils Bohr, the father of quantum theory, had early indicated that in the absence of an observing mind, atoms are not properly real. They only attain a proper reality as they are observed and investigated. Can only scientists get close enough for this effect? Is commonly experienced materiality an illusion created by vast assemblies of ghost-like entities? Because of this possibility of mind-influencing matter directly, Wheeler proposed his cosmology with the Universe attaining to self-awareness through mind. It seems that mind is an indispensable component and the Universe is ready and waiting to work with it. Until mind comes along, the Universe is not properly real.

In such a situation, the strangest of things – strange to the pedestrian intellect, are possible. For instance, Wheeler seriously proposed recently that by appropriate modification of the apparatus in a well-publicised experiment involving photons passing through slits and forming interference patterns on a screen, that it is possible to affect the destiny of the photons *after* they have passed through the slit. This means that human intervention can operate backwards in time: the present affecting the past. This is a good deal stranger than the present affecting the future!

Everett's 'many-worlds' interpretation of quantum theory has lately gained considerable acceptance, in spite of its fantastic implications, for it eases the explanation of certain features, such as the Anthropic principle. When a wave-state of a particle suddenly 'collapses' or changes its state, a multiplicity of different 'worlds' opens up to its successor. These are not merely theoretical worlds, but are deemed to truly exist. But only one can be chosen, and then the others are completely closed off. Presumably in nature, and presumably for almost all of the time, this opting of a particular world is a matter of chance. But as the Universe has gone a very particular way, the Anthropic way, then over aeons of time there must be a faint influence in the choices taken. This suggests that nature is so organised that it is ready for choices to be imposed upon it. This happens with the advent of mind.

The most mind-rattling experiment performed in recent decades in physics, has been the demonstration that the presence of the observer or experimenter influences nature to make a decision when a particle can exist in two opposite states, for example, in left-hand or right-hand spinning. So here is the proof that nature is congenial to being acted upon by mind. In ways not yet properly understood, the mind could well act upon microphysical events with possible eventual effects in the tangible material world. So far this influence of mind has consisted essentially of an intervention or interference in nature. If appropriate meditation, love, desire or other strong emotionalised mind states are brought in, possibly this effect of mind over matter would be all the more decisive. This could be put to experimental testing. Sir Alister Hardy, a biologist of high repute, and other scientists have provided confirmation of such a phenomenon.

Everett's 'many worlds' interpretation of nature may have a particular application to the mind and its destiny. For the mind, like basic reality, operates at field level. Thoughts are not 'things', but like quarks or particles, they occur in an individual mind but have a universalising aspect. When the mind is concentrated upon the material world, thoughts are largely decided by material criteria: by intellect and reason. But in the life of the mind, in creative endeavour, in the dream and in the psyche's destiny in Surreality, a train of thought can be imagined much in the way that the fate of a particle opens up to a plurality of worlds at every 'collapse'. Thought trains do in fact 'collapse', quite suddenly and unpredictably changing. What then happens, is that a multitude of trains of thought opens up into 'many worlds', each very real. For the psyche as a whole this 'many worlds' interpretation of the mind means that the mind takes on the way of nature's working, its 'many worlds' way, and brings innumerable worlds into being at every turn of thought. So it seems that the mind is especially programmed to affect nature by imposing a choice in a 'many worlds' situation.

It must be emphasised that this only occurs at the more fundamental levels of mind, i.e. in the life of the mind remote from material preoccupations. It cannot apply at all to the ordinary, matter-influenced consciousness. But it is the life of the mind which particularly concerns the Universe and its gaining of self-awareness. If this interpretation of mind is correct, it means that the mind's one track line in ordinary existence is an extreme restriction or canalisation of a wide-ranging activity, impossible to grasp or define with its reasoning.

With the mind working in a 'many worlds' way, and a universal field already effectively organised by mind, one can expect that occasionally very strange events will occur in the midst of ordinary existence, as some 'otherness' of mind breaks through. A strange synchronicity of events (strange to ordinary awareness) can be accounted for, as Jung and the physicist Pauli contended, and as the serialisation of time in Dunn's *An Experiment with Time* ingeniously forecast. This important book is now receiving a revived interest. While Jung dreamed of a butterfly, such forces induced a butterfly to appear at the appropriate place on his awakening. Possibly the field could in the future become so powerfully creative that it could even bring a butterfly into existence for the occasion!

Evidently these are very rare events in the present state of things on earth, but as Sir Alistair Hardy and others have noted, and as most people have been made aware at one time or another, strange synchronous events do occur. What seems to bring them about is a particular psychological tension, desire or passion, or some other unclouded contact with Surreality.

CHAPTER 17

Freedom and destiny

Such a concept of mind makes it possible that the past is not merely memory but truly exists, and that the future must in some sense pre-exist. But such an existence, as Nils Bohr affirmed, cannot be of the firm material kind which one would commonly expect it to be. It is a ghost-like, unreal 'future'. Predictability would therefore apply to this vagueness and so would itself be vague, which is quite different from the precise predictions of material events expected of professional seers.

Therefore predicting the future in a firm material sense is not possible – unless unusual mental and field forces could be set to work to force the material future into being, as predicted. From the practical experience of life this simply cannot happen, or happens so rarely that it is of little or no practical relevance. Simple-minded or vulgar prediction, of the kind encountered in the 'zodiac pages' of popular journals and elsewhere, are pure fantasy: placating human vanity or boosting the importance of a material existence in an utterly trivial way. But quite apart from such material predictability, the psychological future of a particular psyche can very likely be predicted, necessarily in a statistical way. What can be intuitively sensed psychologically is more likely to happen than not.

Such a psychological future is not only determined by the innate karmatic constitution of a person, but by forces working upon the psyche from the vast ecology of the field. Many people are aware of a supernal influence or guidance in their lives, at times felt as a definite presence. The painter Paul Klee was convinced of such a guiding presence, which can be summoned by prayer or meditation.

In conclusion, a statistically probable forecast is possible. The optimum can be computed by a particular psyche, taking into account past and present information. This is no more than nature has done in its major evolutionary achievements before the advent of mind, so mind should be much more able to achieve such a computation. Then all that is needed is for the mind to use the universally existing field facilities to influence the future unfolding of material events to comply with such a computation – with positive imaging for instance.

In the foregoing discussion of how the future can be decided by the mind's intervention, it follows that the act of divination by people with sufficiently attuned and powerful minds, may set in motion, here and now, a future field intervention. So that what is forecast will be more likely to happen, which it would not have done had the seer not intervened. This means that we have to take seriously such activities as astrology and divination. The positive side of the coin is that right thinking, right desiring and right anticipation can improve both existing conditions and those of the future.

As intuition is the only guide possible for the prospective seer and the situation in both kinds of predictability are immensely complicated, symbolic strategies have been resorted to from ancient times, providing some sort of matrix in which intuition can operate. It may not matter very much what system is chosen, be it astrology, cards, palmistry, tea leaves, or whatever, although astrology is by far the most sophisticated.

It follows that the material connection or involvement (in astrology, the planetary situation at the time of birth) is incidental, although it may be indispensable for the seer or astrologer to believe that it is decisive. Nor does it matter if the findings are expressed in astrological or other terms. The successful astrologer – and there can be no doubt of a statistical success predominantly at a psychological level – has merely used a particular strategy to tap into the wisdom of the field. Accordingly it would seem that the present flurry of interest in the 'scientific' discovery of connections between the situation of planets and their effects on life and mind, may prove to be a dead end.

The symbols of astrology, like that of alchemy – another subject with significant abilities to tap the wisdom of the field – are archaic. A redefined astrology, as much as a new scientifically acceptable alchemy, is urgently needed.

CHAPTER 18

Fetters and deviancy

The theoretical possibility of a meaningful human transcendence of time, as a partnership in Surreality and Theos, is challenged by lives lived in misery, violence and cruelty, and by other actively dehumanising influences certain to threaten the integrity of the psyche. This contrast between high aspiration and a disheartening failure to be effectively human, is responsible for a chronic and perennial feeling of hopelessness. A sense of sin has haunted human history, which the present day has attempted to dismiss by rejecting all possible meaning in existence.

For much of earth time nature has managed well, preparing the earth for an eventual human emergence and steering perilous courses through frequent near catastrophe, in glaciations and hot-house effects. But the glaciation which began a million years ago, and was most severe about thirty thousand years ago when combined with a plate-tectonic catastrophe, affecting Eurasia, and responsible for the Himalayas, could not be abated. No experience which the earth field involvement had accumulated could counter the devastation of the planet which resulted. Humans were probably originally humanistic, but subsequently intensely dehumanising conditions set in. The earth has now recovered, but with a contaminated post-glacial culture and civilisation.

That humans have persisted in being inhuman in their habits and ways of life, in their individual and social behaviour, is due to the domination of human behaviour by the cortex of the brain, superceding instinct. The cortex has been made especially conditionable to wide-ranging possibilities of behaviour, impossible in the instinctive reaction of all other creatures. This allows human contribution not only to provide the Universe with its self-awareness, but also to be as varied and rich as possible. A rigid reflex pattern of behaviour would be cosmically useless. But in this design, nature made no provision for a dehumanising catastrophe such as an Ice Age. The easy conditionability of the human cortex enabled humans to adapt to the most humanly thwarting conditions: environments robbed of aesthetic meaning and ways of life more debased than that of the beast.

A further device which nature had bequeathed to mankind from the start – the social inheritance of cortical conditioning – has meant that once a cortical pattern was established, it became persistent from one generation to another, irrespective of whether it complied with the Anthropic needs or not. Although variously affected by this planetary deviancy, and periodically lapsing into the demonic and inhuman, civilisation has endeavoured to maintain its humanising resources and the miracle of the human spirit survives.

The emancipatory movements of our times have rightly concentrated on a solution of the material and economic problems of existence, for the transcendental destiny of mankind can only proceed when these challenges have been met. In the past, when the importance of this transcendental destiny was realised, the material and social problems received insufficient attention. Science's dismantling of ancient beliefs and superstition has therefore been salutary. But a scientifically reconcilable meaningfulness must now be restored. Humanism alone, without a supporting belief, has proved inadequate.

Where the emancipatory movements, and humanism in particular, have failed, is to have supposed that on his own man could find a worthwhile existence in a Universe seen as meaningless. Meaningfulness is only possible if an indispensable role can be found for the human in the Universe. But this role has to be earned, given the precarious ways of nature's working. Nothing is secure; nothing is guaranteed. The risks of failure for mankind, as for the Creation, are ever present. To meet the needs of Creation the human being is unavoidably engaged in struggle: in a dialectic between good and evil, between horror and beauty, between purity and impurity. In this struggle, the individual can easily fail. The burden of human responsibility is truly disturbing. The human being is the only creature which has become aware of this situation. Although elected to help the Universe attain its creative goal, threatened by failure and disaster the humans on this planet have added to the risks as much as abated them.

The nature-insensitive and destructive activities of human beings would seem barely believable to superior observers from another world. Mineral resources amassed by earth labours over hundreds of millions of years are being devastated in a few generations. The contamination of the planet with substances completely foreign to life is proceeding at such a pace that it is likely to be irreversible. These are surely signs of a very generalised dementia. Science has overcome some confusions of the past, but it is responsible for a confusion of mind, resulting from its insensitivity and the meaninglessness it has preached. This confusion is as insidious as superstition, for it has paralysed the ability to appreciate the critical human situation in nature. The modern mind, which should be alerted to the fragile range within which alone life can prosper, far from aiding the work of Creation, actively hinders it.

A sense of cosmic responsibility will prove hard to recover. It is not only in deed and action that humans are negligent and destructive. Thought in itself has a supreme power for good or ill. This is not realised because the nature of mind is ignored, together with its place and role in the Creation. If the field guidance theory is correct, then every thought can add to the transcendental accumulation of its power and can influence life for good or ill. No doubt much thinking is ephemeral, lacking wholeness. But as thought acquires integration and relation, so it becomes time-defying.

Wholeness is assured by a humanly sensitive predisposition. But it may have to evolve through strategies which can be humanly threatening. This is seen at work in literary and dramatic art, wherein the human must work with humanly opposing forces – the dialectic in existence which accounts for the appeal of such art. Existential influences are so generalised, that an art which ignores such a dialect is felt as irrelevant and boring. But throughout human history, although the devil has had to be reckoned with, and the demonic given its due, there has usually been reclaim and redemption. Only rarely has the demonic won over. This is well seen in all great literature and drama.

Redemption in the arts, i.e. the eventual victory of human qualities, is essential to their greatness. But conditions can arise when this fails and the demonic runs wild. There is then no human end; love is vanquished; death and suffering are relished. So it is that the arts, and drama in particular, serve as a barometer of the demonic threat. Imageries and music in such times may have a powerfully disturbing effect. But drama probably has a particular sway, owing to its existential connection. In all probability, the creations of personalities and places in drama and literature actually exist in replicate worlds. As we know, every serious writer has been aware that the characters he creates progressively gain a power of their own, and at times, take over. Quite likely, humanly malevolent literature and drama have an actively threatening impact on the work of Creation.

While the great religions have stressed the need for humans to struggle against evil, doubt and contradiction have invariably followed, for how could an all-mighty Creator/Deity permit such evil? Accordingly, ethical demands were obliged to accept human failure, calling for sacrifice and forgiveness – a process often taking terrible tolls. One doctrine which has placed the responsibility for the Creation's success or failure squarely on frail human shoulders is 'high' alchemy. It strove for wholeness symbolised in 'gold', for metamorphic power symbolised in the 'philosophers stone', and for the practical necessity of helping nature in its evolution from an original crudity to an eventual radiant and glorious perfection. In contrast, 'low' alchemy, the most popular, claimed to be able to transmute base metal into gold for venal advantage, and to provide such panaceas as drugs, enabling bodily immortality.

In the past, alchemy was cluttered with symbolisations thought to be meaningless. But it is possible, with advantage, to reinterpret the doctrine in terms acceptable to modern science, especially with the help of the new physics. The subject is of particular interest because it indicates that the sense of human responsibility for nature's success or failure is not a religious preserve, but one depending on an implicit need in nature itself. Religion has in fact tended to confuse this inherent need of a sense of responsibility through its therapies of atonement, forgiveness and the alleviation of guilt through sacrifice. This conceals the terrible fact that there is no outside reference; that man himself is the creative agent, and that the entire onus of Creation falls upon him.

In pre-scientific civilisation, religion endeavoured to serve our higher ideals, but was often distracted by the opportunities of power. As a civilisation becomes aware of the nature of reality and its human responsibility in the fulfilment of Creation, such a religious phase should be naturally succeeded by one marked by individual and social responsibility. It would seem that such a stage is now being entered into. But as the times are transitional, the established practices and beliefs of the great religions can be effective in the same way as meditation. Ritual, music and art can work in the same way. Many of the claims of the great religions, notably Buddhism and Christianity, can be interpreted in the light of the field paradigm, and so be fitted into an emerging self-consistent viewing of human responsibility, nature and cosmos.

CHAPTER 19

The coding of Creation

Cosmologists are now exploring the timeless clues to organisation invested in the universal field and finding the indications of an inception of some kind. That is, of an act of Creation which, if one is to accept the self-consistency of nature, must itself be a natural event. This is not only indicated in the very special way in which the Universe formed during its first few seconds in an orgiastic outburst of energy beyond conceptualisation, but in the way it subsequently expanded and has continued to expand ever since.

Other features point to an original inception of some kind, such as the very special settings of the Anthropic principle. Evolution is not the engineer's or the designer's way of creating a Universe. The evidence of waste and failure are too pressing to allow the belief in some sort of pre-existing plan or design. Like everything else in nature, the Universe has had to grow, by groping, trial and error, from very humble beginnings.

Many people find evolution so awkward that they cannot accept it for what it is: nature's main creative method. Some are so repelled that they simply choose to ignore its irrefutable evidence. Evolutionary theory was acclaimed in the heyday of scientific materialism because Darwin appeared to provide an accidental, mechanistic interpretation of its working. This simple-mindedness is being corrected today. The creative drive behind evolution is staggeringly complex and strange, and will almost certainly need something like the field involvement suggested here to make an overall sense out of it. What could have begun such an extraordinary process?

The awkwardness of evolution is most apparent at the material level. As the material order is penetrated into and the functional approached, one is increasingly confronted with an ingenuity in the basic organisation of nature, as in the Anthropic principle which staggers the imagination. It is in the thrust of this great basic creative wisdom into the making of a material world, that the limitations become apparent. Not only must one assume that the genesis of matter and its laboured evolution in time and space has been indispensable to the Universe, but also that very severe constraints have been imposed from the start. So that whatever started up the Universe could only have done so in the bungling material ways of which we are now aware. In looking around for a creative system which is both ingenious in its inception and awkward in its execution, a Universe that has been coded, rather than directly fabricated, provides the best analogy.

An interesting example of the difficulty of grasping the consequences of decoding a code, and its blind, dogged creative issues, is to be found in reproduction. Sex and breeding motivation are expertly coded into the DNA of the genes; but how few people realise the full implications of their reproductive activities!

Man-made codes can be most ingenious, but for those who do not know the decoding procedure they appear tortuous and baffling. Quite simple codes can provide decoding instructions for the most complex and sophisticated systems. The 'four-letter code' of DNA accounts for life's fantastic outfolding by the intermediary of the subcodes of amino acids. The field involvement, however, may by-pass the DNA gene coding.

One must consider that our Universe could have been initially coded by human-like beings, evidently wiser and more knowledgeable than we happen to be. Universes exist as isolated islands of matter in the universal field, no doubt enclosed by formidable barriers in the nature of enveloping black holes, ensuring their undisturbed entropic identity. The extreme faintness of the 'pregeometry' (which is the code insown into the universal field) and the necessity of matter (so that a functional universe could become organised) were evident limitations imposed by the universal field.

If black holes envelop our Universe, the need for a very faint code can be understood, as anything more assertive would be annihilated. As for what we experience as matter, it is likely to be the outcome of an expressive potentiality of the universal field, which, thanks to evolution and time, becomes organised as form and mass which our senses and intellect interpret in a material manner. But as this special potentiality in the field is realised, giving birth to matter, space and time, so resistance and obduracy result. This is possibly a necessity so as to enforce its mechanical and functional evolution – the means, it will be recalled, of organising the functional Universe.

The numerous coding systems in nature support a coded origin to the Universe itself. The most remarkable coding device is found in the quantum organisation of radiation. This is the primordial coding: the way in which the continuity of the field is given its first discontinuous stamp, resulting in the build-up of distinct material entities. Extremely subtle shifts in this coding account for the visible qualities in nature, such as light and colour, heat and cold, and the variety of human sense organs in response to these properties. As the inhabitants of a Universe become aware of the universe-making process and unravel the code, so they find themselves motivated to create new Universes. This motivation is possibly akin to the reproductive urge, or the urge for adventure and exploration, science and art.

At the moment, we are fast deciphering the code. It is already possible to create new matter from the energy available in our Universe. It should be possible to tap into the inexhaustible supplies of free energy in the universal field, encapsulating the required amount in an enveloping black-hole, thereby providing the evolutionary process of energy into matter with a finite or entropic destiny. To tap into new energies may not be so difficult as one might imagine. Nature itself does so occasionally in the subatomic world, as in the phenomenon known as quantum 'tunnelling'.

Coding from one level of organisation to another, followed by a decoding, is nature's other way of creation besides evolution. Like evolution, it is not readily apparent. This ingenious device means that each succeeding level in nature's hierarchy of organisation brings into being quite new properties which were not apparent at the previous level. For instance, in the jump from the non-living to the living a quite new property, vitality, appears. A property not to be traced reductively to the previous non-living levels.

Such an acquisition of new properties at each emergent level cannot be accounted for in the material mechanisms involved. We must bring in the field involvement, wherein the new properties are first worked out and then played back via the material mechanisms concerned. It is in this manner that the initially extremely faint coding of the 'pregeometry' was successively exploited and amplified, as it was decoded into succeeding levels, gaining in power and resolution.

In the physical realm, the possibilities of this system are limited. The coding and decoding occur initially from the field into the quarks, which then code the elementary particles into being. New levels of organisation come into being as atoms wield energy and interact with gravity, providing the high expertise and guidance in star systems. With the attainment of life, the fantastic coding and decoding of the DNA RNA system comes into play, resulting in those molecular genii, the genes, largely taking on field guidance into living mechanism.

The arts are notably dependent on codes able to decode in symbolic ways with virtually inexhaustible creative possibilities, engendering the most powerful worlds in the replicate order. Perhaps the most astounding application of the coding principle is language. This amazing faculty probably came into being quite suddenly, as a potent replicate direction which had been long and well worked out previously. That it has depended essentially on a field direction with a minimal physiological involvement, is indicated by the virtual absence of specialised parts of the brain connected with language. Only a diminutive area, known as Broca's area, appears to be loosely connected with language.

Thanks to the language code, communication between minds can be highly elaborate and diversified. This is made possible by different languages and dialects, an ingenious way of enriching the mind's contribution to the Universe's own awareness. So rich is the creative potentiality of language that the worlds it has brought into being in mythology, folk and fairy tales, literature and poetry, far exceed the diversities due to DNA. It is no coincidence that language gained an enormous boost from writing and the printed word. For these events coincided with the unfolding of civilisation: the indispensable condition for the emergence of Surreality.

The creation of a new level of organisation by decoding from the codes in a previously existing level, means that what is decoded is not direct, but symbolic. For instance, a quark is not a direct manifestation of field properties, of the 'pregeometry'; it is a symbolic expression of them. Similarly, vitality is a symbolic expression of field qualities especially organised by the material biomolecular systems. This means that the emergence of a material world from a Universe which is basically functional, consists of a staggered, hierarchical symbolising process. At each level the field influence increases. Here is the mechanism, the technique, whereby the Creation can be seen as a work of art, rather than a machine. The mechanical aspects are decisive, for they are the means whereby the field involvement is raised to higher levels. But the creative process cannot be judged from the mechanical aspects. It is the symbolic resolution which is decisive. For as this becomes ever more aesthetically explicit as material evolution proceeds, so the ultimate functional qualities of the Creation become resolved and made manifest.

Our coders should not be conceived of as individuals. At higher levels of social evolution, while individual identity is preserved, space and time transcending participation results in communality which can embrace functionally and effectively not only societies, but planets. A very primitive indication that such a communalisation is built into the fabric of the nervous system and brain can be seen in insects. In hive, anthill or termitary, individuals are unified probably by primitive telepathic means. At higher human levels, a sophisticated space and time transcending force takes over.

In the evolution of the human mind, such intermind phenomena are initially kept down so as to allow individuality to develop. This is indispensable for an optimally diversified contribution to Surreality. The immense creative power of language and the arts could not have come into being if intermind influences dominated. But even in our situation, the tendency for such communalising groups to form can be observed, whether in international cultural relations or those ever-growing teams of scientists working together at international level.

It would seem that one has to accept that the original coders had no means of influencing the process. This only became possible as evolution had got sufficiently under way and the evidence makes it strikingly apparent that some such influence increases. As such an influence grows, so the inter-universe barriers may become progressively fragile. A point would be reached when the coders of a Universe unify with the emerging Theos of such a Universe. This would not only bring the coders to their ultimate fulfilment, but would also bring the Theos into its full power and glory in a supreme 'epiphany'. When this happens the ordinary laws of space and time will be overcome in a total realisation of Surreality.

These suggested methods of Creation may appear tortuous and unnecessarily complicated, but we are without doubt in a very strange place, which is subject to baffling limitations as well as glorious prospects beyond proper appraisal. The reason why we have so often failed to grasp the nature of reality, is that we have longed for a simple explanation; one which our limited rational understanding could grasp. No such explanation is possible.

As to the question of the origin of the entire business of Universe-making, the answer can only be that such questioning is not legitimate: questioning being applicable only to those aspects of reality to which the analytical intellect has access. It has no place in those dimensions of the mind evolved beyond the intellect; dimensions which are most relevant to the Universe-making process. Even in everyday life, the question as to what a work of art is about is not properly answerable; nor can reason ever be found for loving. In the dream, there is never a question of the origin or end of a particular experience. One simply 'is' the experience, and so it is felt to have no beginning nor end.

Of course, the intellect objects that this denial of a right to question is wrong. But a most important corrective to the arrogance of nineteenth-century confidence in the absolute sway of reason and intellect, has been Gödel's demonstration that in mathematics there is an inherent limitation which can never be overcome. While the intellect serves us well in the material realm, and can be extended by such devices as mathematics to go far beyond it, it is limited and cannot, by its very nature, grasp the ultimates.

One must conclude that an understanding of the field involvement in nature, accounting for much, if not all, that refuses to be answered for officially, probably brings the long human search for understanding through the instrument of the intellect as far as it can go, namely, to its coded origins. The scope of the intellect can be extended not only by mathematics but, as has been indicated, by aesthetics and sensitivity and by participation – the latter being the only way in which fundamental events can be experienced. In such experiencing, the human mind is the only instrument available at present; a limitation which will possibly be remedied in the future. But even then, communication will only be possible in symbolically charged ways. This means that science will have to share some of the characteristics of poetry or art. So far, science has rejected such an extension of intellectual knowledge out of hand. And yet, in its present most far-reaching explorations, it has come face-to-face with this limit to the unguided intellect in the discovery of the influence of the 'observer on the observed'. It remains to be seen if there can be such a thing as inspired science, and especially, inspired physics. If not, science as known at present is coming to an end. This would further imply an inbuilt limitation to machine-dependent progress.

It is remarkable how far we have managed to go. This is not so much due to any particular virtue on our part, as to a probable programmed encitement in our minds to thirst for knowledge and understanding, as the means, it will be recalled, whereby the Universe gains such knowledge of itself. Having now gone beyond the confusions and contradictions of the past, we are in a position, in spite of our limitations, to feel a calm confidence in the extraordinary creativity in which we share.

As for the helplessness which the individual is likely to feel when confronted with the deviant and deteriorating conditions on this planet, which rule out any facile optimism, it is helpful to remember that while the purpose of thought is action, thought in a field-involving Universe has a positive effect. Merely to think a thought sets up time-transcending reverberations in the universal field which can acquire a world-changing momentum. Human history is full of examples. While evil can steal into this power transiently, it carries its own eventual disintegration. Whole, humanly related thinking has a timeless and universal capacity. Provided the momentum is sufficient, it is bound to win.

Bibliography

Alexander, S. *Space Time & Deity*, London 1928.

Bohm, D. *Wholeness & the Implicate Order*, Routledge 1960.

Capec, M. *The Philosophical Impact of Contemporary Physics*, Princeton USA 1961.

Davies, P.C.W. *Other Worlds*, Dent 1982.

——*The Edge of Infinity*, OUP 1983.

Dyson, Freeman. *Disturbing the Universe*, Harper & Row N.Y. 1979.

Dirac, P.A.M. ''The Evolution of the Physicist's Picture of Nature'', *Scientific American*, May 1963.

Gale, G. ''The Anthropic Principle'', *Scientific American*, December 1981.

Hardy, A., Harvie, R., Koestler, A. *The Challenge of Chance*, Hutchinson 1973.

Maslow, M. *The Farther Reaches of Human Nature*, Pelican 1973.

Pagels, H.C. *The Cosmic Code: Quantum physics as the language of nature*, Michel Joseph 1983.

Polkinghorne, J.C. *The Quantum World*, Longmans 1984.

Rattray Taylor, G. *The Great Evolution Mystery*, Secker & Warburg 1983.

Rignano, E. *Biological Memory*, Kegan Paul 1926.

Sheldrake, R. ''Formative Causation: the Hypothesis confirmed'', *New Scientist*, 27 October 1983, p.279.

Tang, R., Puthoff, H. *Mind Reach*, Granada 1978.

Waddington, H. *Behind Appearances*, Edinburgh 1969.

Weiskop, V.F. *Knowledge and Wonder*, Heineman 1964.

Wheeler, J.A., Patton, C.M. ''Is Physics legislated by Cosmogony?'', *The Encyclopaedia of Ignorance*, Ed. D. Duncan & M.M. Weston-Smith, Pergamon 1977.

Wilson Avray, F. *Art as Understanding*, Routledge 1963.

——*Alchemy as a Way of Life*, Daniels 1975.

——*Nature Regained*, Boston 1977.

——*Crystal & Cosmos*, Coventure 1977.

——*Art as Revelation*, Centaur 1983.

Zukov, G. *The Dancing of the Wu Li Masters*, Hutchinson 1979.

Index

Current Coventure Titles

Art as Healing* *by Edward Adamson* 0 904575 24 1
The remedial value of creative self-expression, with over 100 colour illustrations by people in Adamson's care.

The Heart Attack Recovery Book *by Elizabeth Wilde McCormick*
0 904575 37 3
A look at the emotional and practical problems encountered during rehabilitation, for patients and their families.

The Baby Massage Book* *by Tina Heinl* 0 904575 15 2
"A gentle, helpful and reassuring book." *Illustrated.*

The New Male–Female Relationship* *by Herb Goldberg*
0 904575 39 X
An immensely encouraging blueprint for a new kind of sexual relationship.

The Challenge of Fate *by Thorwald Dethlefsen* 0 904575 35 7
How life around us reflects our inner nature.

The Unknown Spirit *by Jean Charon* 0 904575 18 7
French physicist Jean Charon explains how "physics has discovered spirit".

The Opening Eye *by Frank McGillion* 0 904575 03 9
The pineal gland and our link with cosmological phenomena.

Relating: An astrological guide to living with others on a small planet* *by Liz Greene* 0 904575 28 4

Looking at Astrology* *by Liz Greene* 0 904576 86 8
A sound introduction to astrology for children. *Illustrated.*

Myth and Today's Consciousness *by Ean Begg* 0 904575 30 6
The mythological expression of forces behind the acceptable face of consciousness.

Germanic Mythology *by Margrit Burri* 0 904575 36 5
The world of myth which belongs to our pre-Roman, pre-Christian, psychic origins.

The Inner World of Childhood* *by Frances G. Wickes*
0 904576 64 7
The fruits of Frances Wickes' practical experience in child psychology.

The Inner World of Choice* *by Frances G. Wickes* 0 904576 66 3
A reprinting of the classic by Jung's longstanding friend and colleague.

Dynamics of the Self *by Gerhard Adler* 0 904576 92 2
Essays on the themes of the psyche, the self and individuation.

In the Wake of Jung *ed. Molly Tuby* 0 904575 23 3
Articles mostly by working analysts, illustrating the practical application and development of many of Jung's ideas.

In the Wake of Reich *ed. David Boadella* 0 904576 58 2
A collection of important papers by colleagues and students of Reich, including Ola Raknes, Gerda Boyesen and A.S. Neill.

The Symbolic and the Real* *by Ira Progoff* 0 904576 63 9
A programme for personal growth.

Mirror to the Light *by Lewis Thompson, ed. Richard Lannoy*
0 904575 19 5
"Poetic aphorisms of great density and beauty" – Lawrence Durrell.

Prospero's Island: the secret alchemy at the heart of "The Tempest" *by Noel Cobb.* 0 904575 26 8
Illustrated.

A Vision of the Aquarian Age* *by Sir George Trevelyan*
0 904576 52 3
A new spiritual worldview for an age stifled by materialistic values.

A Tent in Which to Pass a Summer Night *by Belle Valerie Gaunt and Sir George Trevelyan* 0 904576 35 3
An anthology of poetry and prose concerning reincarnation and the soul.

Magic Casements *by Sir George Trevelyan* 0 904576 91 4
The use of poetry in the expanding of consciousness.

The Psychology of Nuclear Conflict *ed. Ian Fenton*
0 904575 35 7
Insights and views which become a phenomenology of the subjects for professional and general readers.

The Work of Creation *by Frank Avray Wilson* 0 904575 33 0
The aesthetics of art and science to show a wholistic and human-centred creation.

Withymead *by Anthony Stevens* 0 904575 32 2
A Jungian community for the healing arts.

The Grail Legend *by Emma Jung and M.L. von Franz* 0 904575 31 4

Available from Element Books Ltd., Longmead, Shaftesbury, Dorset SP7 8PL. Telephone Shaftesbury (0747) 51339.

*Coventure edition not available in the United States.